*For my parents and siblings,
children and grandchildren*

REACHING FOR THE STARS

I sat on stage waiting my turn. I couldn't really hear the other speakers; their voices muddled around me as my mind revved in anticipation of my speech. I was the final act. I had to light up the stage. Would I make my points? Would my message hit the mark with the audience? I'd been working on this speech for months—my whole life, really. Was I ready? It was too late for second thoughts, too late for regrets. My coach had coached me well, but now it was just me. I had to do it my way.

The emcee welcomed the man who would introduce me. I felt like I was jumping into the unknown, but I knew the fog would clear.

I heard my name. I heard my bio. And then I heard the invitation to tell my story.

"Please help me give an enthusiastic welcome to Jonathan Alcott."

YOU GET OUT OF LIFE
JUST WHAT YOU PUT INTO IT

I grew up in Walnut Grove, Missouri. The sign on the west side of town read "Population 348"; the sign on the east side of town read "Population 350." Either two people died or two were born and they never got around to updating the signs—but this was a minor flaw in the town I loved.

In the 1850s Walnut Grove was called Possum Trot. As you might guess, the name came from the number of possums that inhabited the area. (The town still honors the original name with Possum Trot Days, celebrated late each summer with craft and food stands at Jim Cummins Park.) The town's original site was next to a stand of black walnut trees, and eventually the town became Walnut Grove, incorporating in 1859.

Walnut Grove had two main streets that crossed in the middle of town with a flashing yellow four-way light over the intersection. No need to stop anyone with a conventional traffic light—the traffic didn't warrant it. Homes were spread out within the quadrants. The town had a limited number of streetlights, with one on most corners and none in between.

Businesses lined the downtown streets. At one time Walnut Grove had five gas stations, four grocery stores, a drugstore that sold notions but not prescriptions, five churches, a hardware store, a barbershop, a beauty parlor, a pool hall, two doctors, a fire station and (literally last) a funeral home. Oh yes, and a locker plant where people who didn't have proper refrigeration could store their butchered meat until it was time to use it.

Law enforcement consisted of Town Marshal Robert Fagan and his companion, an old shepherd dog missing a back leg. Fagan didn't own a car, so though not much ever happened in Walnut Grove, when it did, he and his limping dog showed up on foot. But most of the time he and two or three other men gathered in the Missouri Farmers Association store and talked about who they had decided was guilty of something like taking a chicken from Jess Blair's henhouse.

Living in this tiny town in the 1940s and 1950s, I had little opportunity to gain a larger understanding of life. Walnut Grove, located twenty-three miles from the metropolis of Springfield (population 66,000), was a poor town. When I say poor, I don't mean dirt poor, but people did not have money to cover more than the basics of food, doctoring and clothing. Most everyone dressed alike—plain and basic; we children looked like characters from *The Little Rascals* movies.

People worked, and worked hard. We did not take vacations or eat out on weekend nights. We lacked the arts and other forms of cultural entertainment, though the high school offered band concerts and plays from time to time. Television was just coming of age in the early 1950s, and few families could afford one. For that matter, not many folks could afford to take the daily newspaper.

Our family had very little money, perhaps less than most, but we didn't see ourselves as much different from the rest of Walnut Grove's 348 (or 350) inhabitants. In one way we did differ: while most of the homes in Walnut Grove were old and small, my parents had to buy a larger home to accommodate our seven-person family. My dad was a rural mail carrier, and my mom took care of the family. My sister Ellene was the oldest child; then came three brothers, Bill, Lawrence and JE; and I was the youngest of the bunch.

Our house was large, but it was not the Taj Mahal by any means. It was a story and a half with four rooms downstairs—living room, dining room, bedroom and kitchen—and three bedrooms upstairs. My sister Ellene and my oldest brother Bill slept in the back two bedrooms. Lawrence, JE and I slept in the third bedroom. Eventually I turned the large area at the head of the stairs into a fourth bedroom for me.

Downstairs, walls and ceilings alike were covered with wallpaper. In places, the paper had come loose, especially on the ceiling from the heat rising. In the dining room, where we gathered to listen to the radio and then later to watch television, the paper was glued to the ceiling with a flour and water mixture. Since this was not the preferred method of hanging wallpaper, it had to be tacked up while the paste dried. The problem was, no one ever bothered to remove the tacks. Many times I would look at those tacks to remind myself of who we were and our station in life. Yes, I counted the tacks over and over and remember to this day that eleven tacks gave grace to our entertainment room.

Upstairs the cost of hanging wallpaper was spared, and the plaster walls and ceilings were painted in pastel tones. With so many of us kids in the house, the walls were in surprisingly good shape, with one exception: a chunk of plaster was missing on the wall of the staircase. (When I was fourteen, I wanted my home to look better and decided I could fix this problem. I bought a small bag of plaster at Brim's Hardware Store and borrowed a trowel from a neighbor. I was so eager to make a much-needed improvement that I just couldn't believe how bad it looked when I finished.)

The house had pine-board floors that were sanded and varnished; a few hooked rugs were scattered around the downstairs. Registers in the upstairs floors allowed warmth from the rooms below to flow up; there was no other source of heat. On cold nights we piled extra blankets on the beds, and when one of us wasn't feeling well, Mom would warm a brick on the stove, and then wrap it in a towel and put it under the blankets at the foot of the bed. To us kids, that was love.

If the wind blew just right when it snowed, a small snowdrift would form on the windowsill overnight—

though it seemed not to matter much since the whole room was cold. When we woke up, we didn't dawdle; we got out of bed and hurried downstairs where the coal and wood stoves were. I can still feel the chill of that floor on my bare feet on winter mornings. If it had snowed a lot, we listened to the radio for school cancellations; even with chains on their tires, the school buses didn't dare risk the country roads where the rocks and gravel could be iced over.

As was the case with most rural homes, our house lacked indoor plumbing. We had a water pump out back for fresh well water and an outhouse up the hill. On freezing days when I was sent out to pump a bucket of water or, worse yet, had to go up the path to the outhouse, again I didn't dawdle. The outhouse was also called "the privy" or "Miss Hattie." "Gotta go visit Miss Hattie," we would say. We never knew where the name Miss Hattie came from. (Late in life I learned my mother's mother was named Hattie, but I refuse to believe my mother would have called the privy after her mother!)

In my earliest memories our kitchen had an icebox. Two or three times a week the iceman would cometh in his horse-drawn cart. He'd walk through the house carrying a large block of ice to put in the back of the icebox. When we got an electric refrigerator, oh my goodness did we ever stare at it. Wow.

In the pantry off the kitchen stood a tall slender cabinet made of metal. Mom's spices and jars of food fit inside the cabinet's small boxes. On the inside of the metal door was all the parked gum that we kids couldn't part with. There had to be at least thirty wads stuck on that door—nobody ever went back to retrieve their jewel.

The water bucket, with its dipper standing ready, sat on a table in the pantry. On the floor beside the table stood the slop bucket. All the table scraps from the meals were scraped into the bucket along with what water we didn't drink. At some point, one of us carried the bucket up to the pigpen and poured the slop into the hog trough.

As was the norm at the time, we had some livestock to keep us in eggs, milk and meat. In addition to the two pigs who joyfully ate the leftovers from the slop bucket, we had a small flock of chickens and a cow named Molly. We got eggs from the hens, and my mother would wring a feathered neck when it was time for roast chicken. We slaughtered the pigs eventually—I remember those days vividly—with a bullet to the forehead. Whether we had an icebox or electric refrigerator at that point, I don't recall, but we certainly didn't have enough room for a whole hog in our little freezer, so the slaughtered pigs were stored at the cold locker.

My mom got the worst of our lack of plumbing: three meals a day, laundry, washing dishes and bathing all had to be accomplished without running water. If she wanted hot water it had to be heated on the stove. Oh, how she labored and never one time complained.

I learned the philosophy of seeing the bright side of life from my mother. She was a beacon to me, and faced life with an upbeat attitude. I learned that life is what you make it and only you can determine what or who can get into your mind and ruin your day. My mother taught me that when bad stuff happens in your life—and it will— it's not the crisis that's important; it's how you handle it. I saw her happy each day.

And, my, did she love her children, even writing a poem for each of us babes; I still have mine tucked away.

Jonathan...Baby Dear

Many times I've rocked you
when you were a baby dear,
pressed you close to breast
and cuddled you near.

So often your smile has greeted me
from a downy crib,
so many times pearly teeth have flashed at me,
above a snow white bib.

I've guided your little feet in faltering steps,
taught those little hands to pattacake,
been greeted by a precious laugh
the minute you awake.

What are you? Bit of wondrous heaven,
a wee little cuddly Easter bunny
or an angel from soft clouds above,
sent to make the world more sunny?
—Mother

Mom smiled and joked and gave us pet names. My brother Bill was "Willy Bill," Lawrence was "Lawrencie Boy," and JE was "Jakadeeper." I was "Jonny Popper." More than once, as I ran through the house, she would say, "Whoa, galloping gaposis, zip up!" I was always in a hurry and way too busy for zipping up! And she was no weakling: after one particularly deep snowfall, she came out dressed for a snowball fight and fought to get the best of us.

My mother was also known for her witticisms. I asked her one time how to pronounce a word; she told me, and then added that one letter was silent like the "o" in fish. When she was trying to get us all in the car she would say, "All right, you kids, get aboard, and if you can't get a board, get a shingle." She enjoyed these bits of humor more than I did at the time, but today I wish I could hear them all again.

Our mother made many sacrifices for us kids. She never missed a school event. She spent money on clothes for us, but rarely bought anything for herself. Any spare pennies she saved for us—perhaps not much, but a little money to go out on the town. And it wasn't until much later in life that I figured out she didn't really prefer the chicken neck at dinner! But those were minor sacrifices compared to the day-in, day-out work of washing clothes on the back porch, ironing for five men and cooking meals and washing the dishes by hand three times a day.

Mom was always on the go. We had only one car and when she wanted to go somewhere, she had to walk, including to the other side of town to visit friends. She regularly offered her time at school events, at the Ladies Auxiliary and at the church, and especially with the elderly. If volunteers were needed, my mom would be there.

My mother was truly a Proverbs 31 woman: "Who can find a virtuous and capable wife? She is more precious than rubies. ... She extends a helping hand to the poor and opens her arms to the needy. ... She is clothed with strength and dignity, and she laughs without fear of the future. ... Reward her for all she has done. Let her deeds publicly declare her praise." (Proverbs 31:10, 20, 25, 31 NLT)

Church was important to my mother. She took us to the Methodist church every Sunday until we got old enough to fuss about going. It had to be a job to get all of us up, dressed and out the door. At a very early age, I saw politics mixed with religion, who was in and who was out, and I often felt because we didn't attend the Baptist Church or the Christian Church that we were out of the loop. I didn't like it. Nevertheless, to please my mother I went with her every Sunday, and every night I said the prayer that was tacked to the door of the bedroom I shared with my brothers. A card about five inches by eight inches with a blue background displayed the words in glittering silver: "Now I lay me down to sleep, I pray the Lord my soul to keep..."

Between my mother's influence and the pastor's paying a visit to the house, I accepted Christ as my Savior at the age of ten. But even with this rite of passage, I had not truly turned my life over to Him. That would not come for several decades.

As patient as my mother was, I knew I could be a nuisance to her—and quite often I was!

She had a canary, and boy did she want that bird to sing. I came home from school one afternoon and saw that bird perched in its cage doing absolutely nothing. I could almost hear that canary begging me to set it free. I opened the cage and the bird took flight. It landed first on the chandelier and then on top of the drapery rods. Back and forth that crazy bird flew while I tried to figure out how to trap it so I could put it back in the cage.

I saw what was about to happen before the bird made what would be its last landing ever—in the room where the oil stove was located. The stovepipe came up from the back of the stove and then made a ninety-degree turn to connect to the chimney. The poor bird never had a chance. No sooner had it touched down on the hot stovepipe than it fell forward from the shock to its tiny little feet.

Oops. What was I going to do? My mom wanted to hear that stupid bird sing, and it didn't make a sound even as it fell to its death. I had to make the cover-up look real. I put the bird back on its perch, leaning it against the side of the cage and gently tucking its feet underneath it.

I wanted to make it look like it died of a heart attack or other natural causes.

My story didn't fly; my mom knew immediately that I was the reason she would never hear her canary sing.

Mom was not standoffish when it came to confrontations. When she came charging in with her "I've got you, buster" look, we knew there was no need to put up a defense. And she had a standing policy: if any of us got in trouble at school, she would give us equal discipline at home.

One scary day, when I wasn't even ten years old, I learned what she was capable of doing. I watched her in the backyard with the chickens. She picked one up by its head and flung it around. Eventually the body came loose and she was left holding the head. The chicken flopped and flopped and even ran around a little. Suddenly, I saw my mother in a totally different light. I thought, *I'm not messing with her!* I knew when she said that if we got punished at school we would get the same treatment at home, she meant it.

When she asked me about a particular offense, I usually just said "Yes" to get the punishment over with as quickly as possible. Most often I received a tongue-lashing. In grade school, the kids liked to compare notes about family behavior. I remember several boys all agreed that they would rather have a whipping than a scolding. I thought, *You're nuts! I'm not into physical pain.* The other way she doled out punishment was to say, "Jonathan, we need a fresh bucket of water." Sigh. Time to trudge up the hill. In some parental way this penalty gave her satisfaction that she was teaching me a lesson.

My mother was not one to whip me at every turn, but one winter night at the supper table I felt her hand of discipline.

I had developed a habit of always saying "Huh?" to every question, even when I knew full well what was said to me. Well, she must have had enough of my "Huhs." She said, "Jonathan, if you say that one more time I'm going to backhand you!" I heard her loud and clear, but habits die hard, and some habits take longer than others to die out.

Mom, Dad, Lawrence, JE and I sat at the dinner table. Mom had fixed chili for supper to warm us up that cold night. Now in a family of our size, we sometimes had to add seating to the table in rather unfashionable ways. Since I was the littlest, my seat was a small empty nail keg with a pillow on top.

My mom got up from the table to get everyone a refill on milk and said, "Jonathan, do you want some milk?"

You know what happened next without my telling you. Out of habit I said, "Huh?"

I never saw it coming! Since the nail keg was so low, I was on the floor looking up before I knew it. I don't even remember falling to the floor. All I remember is lying there and hearing my brothers and my dad laughing. That sound hurt more than the hit.

I never said "Huh" again.

My mother's life was something of a mystery. As with many of her generation, she kept her private life private.

Growing up, I knew that my mother and her brother Clarence had been adopted by the Watson family and her brother Bill had been adopted by the Vetter family. My mother was adamant on how she felt about her adoptive parents—how wonderful they were, how good they were to her, how fond she was of them. She called them Dad and Mom. But the Watsons had died by the time I came along, so I never knew my adoptive grandparents. When I asked about my biological maternal grandparents, I got evasive responses.

At school I would listen to other kids talking about their grandparents; some even had a grandmother or grandfather living with them. I didn't say a word. I wondered what it would be like to have that affection. I wanted a stronger connection with the past, a better understanding of my parents. Of course, I couldn't have said it in those words at the time, but I somehow knew I was missing out—missing out on stories and family.

My mother's life had a second mystery that drew more flippant non-answers: her first marriage to a man by the name of Heying. Why had she divorced? "He would bring toilet paper home in his lunch box." Yes, I had a mother who had divorced in the 1920s—a time when divorce was much less common and much more scandalous than it is today. I got the impression that her husband cheated on her, though she never said for sure.

But I did know that my mother's first marriage provided me a half sister, Dorothy Heying.

My half sister, Dorothy, was nineteen years older than I was. Growing up, I don't remember her being around much; when she did come home, she didn't stay long. However, around the time I was born, she still lived at home and attended Walnut Grove High School; I have a picture of her on the school steps with her classmates.

From bits and pieces of many varying stories from equally as many storytellers, I gathered Dorothy traveled a rocky path in life, largely by her own choice. She became pregnant out of wedlock at age fifteen. My parents did not want this to be known in the small town of Walnut Grove and sent her to my Uncle Bill's home in Republic, Missouri, to have the baby. Dorothy gave up her son for adoption. She then married a young man who went off to the Korean War; they divorced when he returned.

Dorothy's fortune seemed to change when she married Richard Farrington, an attorney in Springfield. His father was a Missouri Supreme Court Judge, and Richard earned his own ranking in the legal system by virtue of some big cases he won. The Farringtons were politically important people in the Missouri Democratic Party, and their picture was often in the society section of the Springfield newspaper, the *News & Leader*. Dorothy was a beautiful lady with blond hair, an equally pretty smile and a charming personality. Socially sharp, she knew the dos and don'ts of what was proper and ladylike. (I think I might remember all of six things she taught me about social manners.)

Dorothy and her husband lived in a new area of Springfield that required a substantial investment. The really exciting difference between their home and ours was they had an indoor toilet and we had an outhouse that also served as a rifle target. (Put that in the society section and watch the envy grow!) They belonged to a private country club, where Dorothy played tennis regularly; both were avid golfers, even playing with Payne Stewart on occasion.

I can imagine how Dorothy felt about her elevation to this lofty place in society. This new life was beyond anything she could have imagined as a young girl. However, we were not made to feel a part of Dorothy's life. I imagine this was related to social status; we poor relations would be like fish out of water in that world. If this ever troubled my mom, she never ever mentioned it.

Perhaps not all was as smooth sailing as it seemed though: Dorothy became an alcoholic and drank for many years, and her distance from the family continued.

On the other hand, Ellene, my "full" sister and the oldest of us five, was as close as a sister could be—sixteen years older than I, she was practically a second mother to me. She had a sweet heart and gentle spirit. I loved to hear

17

her laugh, high pitched and sincere. My sister expressed herself with great clarity, and was not to be taken lightly when her mind was made up. She knew exactly what she wanted and said so.

When I was little, Ellene had the back bedroom upstairs and sometimes I liked to sleep with her. On one of these occasions I happened to have gotten a new pair of lace-up shoes. Back in those days getting new shoes was a very big deal, and I did not want to take off my new shoes at bedtime. My mother took my side of the argument while my sister pleaded her case for shoe removal. I overheard my mother tell Ellene that when I went to sleep she could take my new shoes off. My mom had switched sides in this battle! But I would outflank my sister and Benedict Arnold mom; I would show them. I was determined to stay awake for hours. In reality, fifteen minutes later I had winked out, and off the shoes came. What traitors!

After high school Ellene married Grant Burros, who worked for Trailmobile, and they had five children. (The nights were cold; maybe they didn't have a television!) Those kids kept Ellene busy all day long. The family rented a house on Shorty Thompson's place, not far from us; I would cut across three different fields to go visit. I grew up loving those kids. I say "kids," but I wasn't that much older than they were. I often spent the weekend at Ellene's home and loved playing with my nieces and nephews.

Every Sunday after lunch Ellene and her family came over to our house for a visit. I always watched for them to drive up. Naturally this was before seat belts, and at least three kids would be standing up in the rear, hanging over the back of the front seat eagerly waiting for the trip to end. The visits consisted of much running around the house and games galore: hide-and-seek or magic tricks or pushing the youngsters on the tree swing my brothers had put up. Shortly after supper Ellene and her husband started rounding up the kids to go home. The house grew silent, and I felt mysteriously alone. Years later I would recognize this feeling again when my own children left home.

While my sister Ellene always called me Jonathan, my three brothers—Bill, Lawrence and JE—called me JP, for Jonathan Pryor. Lawrence had started calling me JP when I was little, and it stuck.

My brother Bill, who was nine years my senior, showed an interest in me and nurtured me not only as an older brother but as a mentor. After he graduated high school, he went to work in Wichita. I remember one time when he came home for a visit, he lifted me up to the roof of the coal shed on the back of the garage. We sat up there and ate sandwiches and had a little "man" talk. I felt special to have someone so much older spending time with just me.

I was closest to my brother Lawrence. Six years older than I, he was the brother who, along with my sister Ellene, took the most care of me. When I was in the first grade, I often missed my mother and would go looking for Lawrence in another schoolroom. When I found him, he would gently lead me back to my room with words of comfort and encouragement.

While my brother JE was the closest to me in age, only four years older, we weren't very close emotionally. Matter of fact, sometimes I thought JE didn't even like me. Once when I was wandering the school in search of Lawrence, I found JE instead. Rather than the kind help Lawrence gave, I received a disgusted look. The first time I filled out a job application I listed my name as "Little Idiot" because that's what JE called me. (Joke! Joke!) Oh, JE tormented me as a child—then again, perhaps all brothers torment each other. JE, though, seemed to have been born filled with anger, and none of us ever developed a close relationship with him. In some ways JE reminded me of my father.

My father, William Lawrence Allcock, was from Monett, Missouri, close to Republic. His parents, Jonathan and Elizabeth, died before I was born; I was named for his father.

(You may note, dear reader, that the name on this book is not Jonathan P. *Allcock*, but rather Jonathan P. *Alcott*. After withstanding years of jokes about the name

Allcock, in the mid-1970s, my brother Bill decided to take my father's middle name as his last name; instead of Bill Allcock, he became Bill Lawrence. Then JE changed his last name to Lawrence, too. My wife at the time encouraged me to change my name as well; however, I wanted my name to remain close alphabetically, so I chose the name Alcott. Lawrence faced a conundrum: he couldn't very well pick the last name Lawrence or he would become Lawrence Lawrence. He could keep the name Allcock, choose my last name Alcott, or find another name all together. He chose Alcott. So we ended up four brothers, two with the last name Lawrence and two with the last name Alcott.)

From my earliest years I recall my dad's odd sense of humor. "Jonathan," he said, "did you hear about the Indian chief who drank tea all day long?" Naturally I said no. Then he finished with the punch line: "Well, they found him floating dead in his tea pee the next morning!" Groan.

When I was about eight years old, my father took JE and me fishing. When we got to the river my dad put a worm on my hook and helped me toss the hook in the water. He turned to JE and said, "If he catches a fish he'll get sick at his stomach." Sure enough, I caught a little sun perch and suddenly I vomited. I guess it was the excitement of catching my first fish ever. The two of them had quite a chuckle over that.

My dad did not, however, have a sense of humor about croquet. He loved croquet. He played in area tournaments and was considered quite good. With our croquet set, we kids played War more often than we played a regular game. War was simple: you merely knocked someone else's ball as far as you could. My dad did not like to see our lack of seriousness toward his favorite game.

I always knew something had upset my dad when he used certain phrases. When he and my mother would get in a heated debate, at the height of the argument my dad would shout "Hell's bells and panther tracks!" as though he were a statesman, thumbs hooked in the sleeve holes of his vest, telling my mother the way it was going to be. This puzzling phrase brought laughter to us kids; we knew it was nothing more than bluster. And when he was exasperated over a matter that was out of his control or was going to cost him money (or both, like the time JE hit a baseball through the pantry window), we'd hear "Ye gods and little catfishes!" reverberate throughout the house.

Bad jokes and puzzling exclamations notwithstanding, my father was very intelligent. Both my parents attended school only through third grade, but they were not dummies. You rarely saw either without book in hand, and my father often dispensed wisdom. "If you learn a new word every day, Jonathan," he would say, "you'll know the whole dictionary by the end of your life." "If you lift a seventy-pound calf and continue lifting it every day as it grows, you'll be able to lift a full-grown cow." Or when he begrudgingly gave us a quarter: "Don't spend it all in one place."

My father was never a particularly social man. He went to the VFW and Ladies Auxiliary meetings, but never attended church or came to our school events, not even graduation. Mom, on the other hand, never missed an event. But if she wanted to go somewhere, she had to get a ride or walk—Dad didn't want to go or didn't care enough to take her. As a matter of fact, the only time I remember being in the car with both my parents was the time a train car jumped the tracks; since my dad was interested in railroads, we drove to where the incident happened. Sometimes as I was walking home from school, my father would drive by after completing his mail route. He would honk the horn at me but not stop. Just a little *beep-beep!* One time I flagged him down. Oh boy, Dad didn't like that, but I hopped in anyway. I never did that again.

BEFORE YOU CAN BE OLD AND WISE, YOU MUST BE YOUNG

Despite my father's taciturn nature, the house was filled with fun when my sister and all my brothers were there. We spent a lot of time outside doing one thing after another. We wore dirt trails into the grass around the house. The ground was bare where we played baseball and football. And we had a basket we used as a basketball hoop to play HORSE. When we couldn't find a basketball needle to pump up a slightly deflated ball, we learned we could put it on the wood stove for a short time to inflate it. While only a short-term fix, this method could keep the game going until a winner was declared.

It stood to reason that a similar technique could be used for a flattened ping-pong ball so we could continue our games of "front porch baseball," which consisted of hitting ping-pong balls up the side of the house. (If you hit the porch roof, you made it to first base; the next roof was second base, and so on. Hitting a ball over the house counted as a home run, though few homers were ever hit.) Instead of repairing our ping-pong ball directly on the stove, we brought a small amount of water to a simmer and then dropped the ball in for five seconds.

Fixed! The game could resume. This gentle competition resulted in little damage to the house, except for the time the burner didn't get turned off and almost welded the small pot in place. We were ordered to stay out of the kitchen if our sole purpose in being there was to enhance our sports activities. Almost all the blame fell on my older brothers; I was just a young, "innocent" bystander.

Another front-porch game was choosing a particular make of car and seeing who "won" by how many cars of your choice passed by. My brothers always chose Fords and Chevrolets, while I ended up stuck with the less popular Buick or Plymouth. Guess who always won? We made the game a bit tougher by adding a second selection of whether the driver was male or female. Then it got even harder: did the car hold two males? two females? two females and one male? You get the idea. With this level of complexity, our game went on life support and soon expired.

When not in school, I often rode my bike to town, exploring the side streets and alleys. I had almost too many things to do and see. Sometimes friends and I would ride over to Kenny Wheeler's drugstore to watch his television, for many years the only one in town. At first, the antenna on the roof picked up only one channel, and the only show of interest we could find was wrestling, which often featured a blond, curly-haired guy called Gorgeous George. On occasion I came across the fire truck extinguishing a small fire, generally a grass fire that got out of control when someone was burning trash or a small shed that caught fire when kids were smoking behind it (not that I ever missed the chance to attend a behind-the-shed event as I got a little older). But I didn't need to find an alien spaceship landing or an armed robbery taking place; I just wanted to observe the world and dream of my unknown future as I rode.

Being the youngest had its privileges, but it also had its drawbacks—especially with regard to my brothers. I never understood how those three could come up with so many (what seemed at the time) torturous games.

My brothers loved to call me to come play outside. Well, when I heard them call my name it was like a salt lick for a deer; I couldn't wait to get outside and join a new game or see why they wanted me. My eagerness was quickly taken apart and dismantled field-rifle style. Sometimes they would be waiting for me on the edge of the porch roof, ready to drop burlap sacks full of leaves or balloons filled with water on me. Other times they got me down on my back and straddled me while leaning over my face. Once in this position, they let the slobber accumulate on their lips, slowly let it *almost* fall in my face, then quickly sucked it back up. Except they didn't always suck quick enough.

My brother Bill did the worst thing ever (I remember it like it was yesterday). Bill pinned me on my back—and let a granddaddy long-leg spider walk on my face! My screams finally brought my mother to the door. Oh I was looking for him to get a punishment that equaled the crime, something like hanging maybe, but all he got was a stern command to let me up. So much for justice. That was enough to cause any boy of eight to walk away thinking his mother didn't love him.

Bill eventually redeemed himself by bringing me a replica of a tarantula from a trip to Texas. It looked surprisingly real with a hairy body and legs made of small tight black springs that moved when touched. It appeared ready to jump. One day I put it under the bedspread on my mother's bed, and then proceeded to forget all about my prank until I heard her scream that night.

I always wanted to be buddies with my older brothers—when they would let me. On weekends the radio was usually tuned to a baseball game. My dad was a Phillies fan; my three brothers were Cardinals fans. In the beginning, I joined in with my brothers so I could root with them over hits and outs. I regretted abandoning my dad though, and one day I made the mistake of saying I was a Phillies fan again. My dad found my newfound love of the Phillies humorous, but my brothers decided I needed to be taught a lesson. They informed me I could not come back to the Cardinals. At that age, I swallowed their edict hook, line and sinker. I believed they held the ultimate power of preventing me from being a Cardinals fan ever again. It wasn't long before I chose not to care one way or the other—better to let it go than to pine after something they wouldn't let me have.

As my siblings got older and treated me better (tortured me less!), I had a great childhood. There were rarely any boring times when we were all together, but there were lonely times when they were all off somewhere else and I was left behind.

Saturday nights were especially lonely. My brothers would get cleaned up and put on freshly ironed shirts and Levi's with well-defined creases down the legs (which my mother had labored over) so they would look their best. They slicked their hair back with Brylcreem, and a heavy splash of Old Spice signified all was ready for a night of fun. I would stand at the door as they left and watch them until they were out of sight. The smell of Old Spice lingered in the air for some time, well after they had gone. I always felt left out. It seemed like the words I heard most often from them were "You're too young and too little, so you can't go."

Left on my own so much, I spent a lot of time in my head. Across the gravel road on the other side of the neighbor's house stood a giant maple tree. I'd sit under it and dream about growing up, about becoming successful. Of course at ten or eleven years old, I had no idea what "success" really meant. One can't know what the color red looks like until one sees it. How could I know what success looked like when I lived in a town where people had to strive so hard for life's bare necessities, let alone anything beyond?

To me, success was more a feeling. My heart started racing and excitement rose as I thought about this vague concept. I didn't know what I wanted to do, but I knew I was going to achieve it.

I lived on those feelings. I lived on those dreams. I lived in my mind. And I learned to be happy alone with myself.

Summertime and the living was easy. Lazy days with no school, biking around town, playing baseball in the yard... And what would summer be without swimming?

We went swimming at a river east of where we lived; the swimming hole was called Big Rock owing to the big rock on one side of the bank. (Original, huh?) Swimmers would climb up on top of the big rock and jump in the river. Someone—I'm sure it was a boy—tied a heavy wire cable to a limb that stuck out over the big rock. Most youngsters found it impossible to resist the risk of swinging out and turning loose at the right moment. If you swung out too far and let go, you ran the risk of dropping onto the gravel bar; if you dropped too soon, you landed on rocks at the base of the big rock. You had to time it just right to hit water. I must admit I never tried the cable—I believe in self-preservation! But I did follow the other Big Rock tradition: hanging my swimming trunks on the car antenna to dry in the wind on the way home.

Summer nights were filled with fun too. Friday nights the school band played in a vacant lot downtown, and the Lions Club or the VFW provided a free ice cream social. (It was all about the free ice cream cone for me!) Parents came to listen to the music, meet old friends and let the kids play.

On a good night there might be eight of us kids running around the sidewalks and alleys, hollering and having so much fun it almost took our breath away. When we reached that crazy level, we knew it wouldn't last much longer. I never quite understood that phenomenon as a kid: about the time you got all wound up, it was time to stop. The enemies of fun were the dreaded words "You boys settle down!" or "Come here and sit down!" and the very worst of all: "It's almost time to go home!" Life was over; it would never be the same again. Nope, once those words were out there, it was impossible to bring them back. That's what being a parent is all about I suppose—killing fun.

Summer's highlight was the Fourth of July. I loved Independence Day. We would go to Gene Lemon's service station to get a large block of solid ice. The man there would open the door to a small house about the size of a playhouse with no windows. The walls were thick with insulation, and sawdust covered the large cubes of ice to help keep them frozen. The man used a pair of ice hooks, which looked like large salad tongs with sharp points, to pick up a cube for us and place it in the car trunk where my dad had spread newspaper.

When we got home my dad carried the cube along with the newspaper out to the pump to rinse off the sawdust. Then he put the cube in a big washtub and used an ice pick to chip away at it until the large piece of ice had become a bunch of irregular shapes. Next, he filled the tub of chipped ice with soda pop. Not only did it excite me to see that much pop in one place and within my reach, the real thrill was the rainbow of orange, grape, strawberry and Coke. Spectacular! My mom would make bologna or Spam sandwiches and potato salad. Then we feasted and waited for darkness so the fireworks could begin.

To create a rocket launcher, my dad took one of the small hog troughs, knocked off one end, and leaned it against the fence. We had Roman candles that shot balls of fire out the end of the tube. The rule was clear: all fireworks were to be pointed upward. However, my brothers were known for breaking the rules. While my parents were around, we aimed the rockets up and toward the train station, though they always fell short and landed in our field. Once Mom and Dad had gone inside, Lawrence and JE would each frantically grab a Roman candle and quickly light the fuse—speed determined who was forced to retreat while being shot at with flying fireballs. I tended my sparklers and enjoyed the delicious smell of sulfur from all the fireworks.

With the intuition of a child, I could tell by the slowing of excitement when it was time to go in the house. The Fourth was over for another year.

But there was plenty of summer left, and summer meant good watermelon eatin'. Watermelons were not always on hand like they are today, and it was a treat when my dad would go to town to buy one. Most of the time we went to the locker plant where a man would lead us into a very cold walk-in cooler. He'd "plug" the melon by taking a knife and cutting a small tapered triangle shape into it. Then he'd stick the point of the blade in the center of the wedge and pull it out for my dad to test it for sweetness. I don't ever remember a watermelon being rejected.

I'm not sure which was more exciting: the idea of getting a watermelon or the experience of being in such a huge cold room. I knew more excitement was on its way, though. Later in the afternoon, all of us went out in the side yard, where we had plenty of shade and plenty of seating. My dad settled in his Adirondack chair with a saltshaker resting on the wide arm so it was within close reach.

We held the slices in our hands, leaning forward so the juice wouldn't drip on our clothes. My mom and Ellene were always careful and mannerly in discarding the seeds from their mouths. My dad was, too, but not like Mom and Sis. My brothers, on the other hand, thought it was cool to see who could spit the seeds the farthest. It wasn't long before they were directing them at one another and ultimately at me, the prime target. Mom, as always, came to my rescue, while my dad laughed.

When summer ended and school began, I readjusted my routine reluctantly. But at least I had Christmas to look forward to.

I know I am not unique in saying I loved Christmastime, but I did.

I can still smell the cedar tree that my older brothers would chop down and bring into the house. My mom started the decorating process, and then handed it over to us kids. She assigned us the task of putting the tinsel "icicles" on the tree, though as the fun wore off, they ended up being tossed on in clumps. The aroma of Christmas dinner being cooked — turkey, dressing and all the trimmings — filled the whole house. There was a feeling in the air that our world was all-perfect and the family lived in total harmony. It was partly because of the Christmas spirit, but mainly because my mom made this a very special time for us all.

Each Christmas Eve my mother would put out a snack for Santa: a couple of saltine crackers on a saucer and small glass of milk, set on top of the radio in the living room. Then Christmas morning she followed a strict protocol, a method I liked very much. She lined us up at the closed door that led from the warm dining room into the living room, where the tree was lit and the presents carefully placed under it. We stood according to our age, which meant I got to be first. When everyone was in position and had settled down, she said, "Jonathan, go on in," as she opened the door.

The first thing I checked out was the crackers and milk; Santa always left behind some cracker crumbs. Next, my mother would pass out the gifts, and we would tear into them like wild dogs.

We didn't get many gifts, maybe three or four each. My half sister, Dorothy, always gave each of us kids a huge Hershey's candy bar that we spent the first day just holding and looking at. So much chocolate in one place was beyond understanding; we knew no store in Walnut Grove sold such a monster of a candy bar. We usually got one or two toys, and the remaining presents would be socks or some type of clothing necessary for school.

Many things we got for Christmas didn't last long; they would break or lose their appeal and be discarded. But my most cherished Christmas gift I still have to this day: when I was sixteen, my mother gave me a two-volume desk set of encyclopedias signed with the date and her name, with love.

My interest in collecting started at a very early age. At nine years old I began collecting old keys—keys that didn't lock or unlock anything, or at least not any locks I could locate. They were keys with character defined by their shape, patina, engraving, rarity and mystery. I imagined a special key that would unlock something unbelievable, something no one had ever seen before. I never found that key.

My second collection was marbles. I had marbles of all different colors and types: glass, cat's eye, devil's eye, beach ball and my favorite, onion skin, which was German-made and extremely rare for a kid in Walnut

Grove. When I saw a type of marble I didn't own, jealousy reigned.

When I began collecting arrowheads, I visited newly plowed fields, which yielded the best chance for finding arrowheads freshly brought to the surface. I'd spend afternoons walking up and down the rows, eyes scanning the ground. What an exciting moment to spot a glistening white rock resting comfortably on top of a furrow. This is when I learned what collecting was all about. The hunting, the decision: what was worth adding to the collection, and what was not? I was hooked.

Being a collector must run in the family. My dad was serious about collecting model railroad trains. Ellene loved to collect porcelain figurines, mostly religious ones. My brother Lawrence collected old Coke items, and my brother JE collected antiques. Only brother Bill didn't catch the collecting bug. And then there was my mother...

My mom had a very large collection of salt and pepper shakers. The majority of her collection came from friends, and she would not part with a single set. She had sets that represented every state in the union as well as sets from countries around the world. She arranged them neatly in several stacked barrister bookcases and highlighted a special set of two little brown churches that looked like "The Little Brown Church in the Vale," her favorite Rosemary Clooney song.

One particular pair of shakers caught my eye: two small bottles of Tipo Chianti. One contained real red wine and the other real white wine. After school I would look at those bottles, thinking I could add red cake coloring to a little water, swap it out with the red wine, and no one would be any the wiser. One afternoon, I decided to give it a try. Had I really thought this whole thing through I would have done a color test ahead of time. After some failed colored-water attempts, I thought I had a near perfect match, but later I would realize that my mom's ability to see into the unknown was very much alive. The worst thing was, I discovered the idea of wine was much better than the actual wine. I ended up pouring it out.

I still have several sets of her collection in a display case in my kitchen—including the two empty miniature wine bottles. They make for a great conversation piece. More important, they remind me of my mom.

Growing up, my brothers and I all had guns. My older brothers hunted mostly for squirrels and rabbits, sometimes for deer or quail. My biggest game were squirrels and rabbits, for target practice more than anything.

At that time, if you wanted a special gun, say a Marlin, then you saved your money and bought it for your own, but guns weren't something you got or were given; they just were always there. The only gun control came from your mom and dad or maybe an older brother. Safety was handed down from generation to generation, along with good common sense. You never fired into the unknown; you didn't even think about it.

Sometimes, though, you'd think we took lessons from Marshal Fagan.

Rumor had it Fagan had left the Kansas City Police Department because he had cracked a gangster case and his life was in danger. Now from where I sat, Fagan just didn't fit the profile of a top-notch, big-city detective. He was overweight and dragged his feet. He slumped a bit to the right, which was accentuated by his gun pulling down his khaki pants on that side. Would a big-shot officer really come to our little town just to clean up drunkenness, street gambling and brawls?

Fagan was known for some decisions that would equal Barney Fife or—worse yet—the Apple Dumpling Gang.

One winter, a car sped through town every night at a hundred miles an hour. Without a vehicle, Fagan could offer no chase. After several nights of frustration, Fagan finally caught the speeder by listening for the loud exhaust pipes as the car approached; then he stood in the middle of the road with his gun pointed directly at the driver.

Another time, a shoplifter stole a couple of items from Brim's Hardware. Fagan happened by just as the store clerk stuck his head out the door yelling, "Thief!" Fagan quickly pulled his pistol and started firing at the crook's heel as he ran away. The crook took refuge under a car that was parallel parked not far down the street. Fagan did his best to get the man to come out, with little success. Finally an onlooker said, "Why don't you just get Harold to pull his car off of him?" After the puzzled look left his face, Fagan ordered the car to be pulled forward. It revealed the shoplifter lying there with his hands across his chest, looking as though he'd been carefully laid out by Brim's Funeral Home.

When three men from the nearby quarry town of Phenix came to Walnut Grove drunk and raising Cain, Fagan showed up with his dog and loaded gun. The men began attacking Fagan, and he reached for his blackjack (as we called police batons in those days). The three men quickly wrestled the blackjack from his hand, but Fagan was not going down easily. He pulled out his pistol and started firing, anywhere and everywhere. The men ran behind a car with their hands up. Fagan continued to shoot. Ernie Jones ran out from the storefront where he'd been watching and, without thinking, held his hand up in front of Fagan's gun. "They're trying to give up, Fagan!"

None of us boys was free of the occasional Fagan-esque incident.

One fall day my three brothers and a friend, Howard, took their guns into the woods to shoot some squirrels, or maybe a rabbit if one popped up. I got to tag along even though I was still too young to use a gun. After "hunting" for a while, we sat on logs in the dry riverbed talking and swapping stories.

My brother Bill sat across from Howard at a distance of about five feet. Bill said, "Howard, pick up that hedge apple and put it on your head, and I'll shoot it off!" Well, believe it or not, Howard did, and my brother, without thinking, raised his .22 caliber pistol and cleanly knocked the apple off with the shot.

The gun cracked loudly, but the silence that followed was even louder. Everyone was stunned, and the two most stunned were Howard and my brother. We spent the next several minutes in awkward speechlessness.

Finally, someone said we had better head on home. Little was said on the walk back, but every few minutes someone would mumble a barely audible comment under his breath and a little chuckle would surface from the group. I took this as their way of calming their fears of what could have happened.

My Fagan-like story? When I got old enough to shoot a gun, I joined my brothers in using the outhouse door as a target with our .22 rifles. One day I was getting ready for a little target practice. I had just leveled the gun off, ready to pull the trigger; I could feel the spring giving way to my squeeze. Then I noticed the door was closed too tight for the privy to be empty.

As I started to lower the gun for a more careful look, my mom came out the door. My heart sank to my toes. I almost killed my mom.

I never shot that gun again.

For reasons not altogether clear, my father's already-limited social participation ended completely by the time I was nine or ten. He became very withdrawn and almost non-existent in our lives. He was physically present but uninvolved, silent and disconnected. One year my mother went so far as to ask the guy at Wheeler's drugstore to attend the annual father-son banquet with Bill as a stand-in for my father. How humiliating for Bill, for Dad—even for me. What did that say about us as a family?

I remember my father from when I was very young as a happy and engaging person, and I know he was happy at some point before I was born. He'd bought home-movie equipment, and I could see from the films of that young family how different he was from the father I knew most of my life.

By this time, my parents didn't interact. Each night Mom had dinner on the table at six o'clock and we ate largely in silence. Oh, we boys might talk to Mom (Ellene was married and gone by this time), but Dad didn't say much at all. No one discussed family issues unless one of us did something wrong; even then the reprimand was private. When Dad finished eating, he got up and left the table. I helped Mom with the dishes; sometimes I dusted or vacuumed. Then we filled the evening with radio or television (still great tools for blocking communication). Dad went to bed around 9 p.m.; he slept in a room upstairs, and my mother slept downstairs.

This was the routine. It was a burden.

We all felt the unrest around my dad. We never exactly saw him misbehave, but we rarely brought friends home. We didn't know what Dad might say; we felt uneasy and embarrassed. I grew up always feeling I was *different*. I longed for the way things *should* be—Ozzie and Harriet.

I'm not sure what triggered the change in my father; I can only guess it was related to a health condition he suffered. My father developed an apparent allergy. His face got red, scaly and swollen; his eyes became slits. It got so bad, he went to the VA hospitals in Springfield nearby and further away in Fayetteville, Arkansas, for treatment.

Was it a reaction to weeds? Livestock? Did his skin react from leaning against the cow while milking her? Out of an abundance of caution, and having no place else to start, we got rid of the animals. I liked having livestock and was sad to lose my pseudo-pets; I still have the cowbell Molly wore around her neck.

The precautions didn't seem to help. Dad didn't go out much—only to and from work or up the path to the privy. He didn't sleep well; he had to sleep propped up in bed. He no longer fished; he couldn't sit out in the yard in his Adirondack chair. Everything stopped.

The doctors at the VA never could say for sure just what caused the rash. Each year he would go to the hospital for a week or two. When he came back he had velvet smooth skin, unbelievably new and almost not real-looking.

I think, or maybe hope, that this was why he was the way he was. But in a family that doesn't communicate, you don't even get to hear a lie.

SUCCESS IS A JOURNEY, NOT A DESTINATION

We were friends with two brothers who lived about a mile and a half from us, Gary and Wayne Head. Even as a young boy, I knew that they didn't have a functioning family, though of course I wouldn't learn that phrase until much later in life. Gary and Wayne's parents were country and western singers; their real last name was Head, but their stage names were Sue and Shorty Thompson. Sue and Shorty traveled much of the time performing and left the boys at home alone, even as young as twelve and ten. Gary and Wayne had to get themselves fed and get themselves to school. They didn't have so much as a grandparent there to take care of them. Wayne and I buddied up since we were the youngest ones. Gary was closer to JE's age.

Wayne was a good, well-adjusted kid. He treated me nicely, always a pal. We rode horses together, walked to football and basketball games together, and talked about girls when we got to high school age. I knew if I needed bully protection I could call on Wayne.

Gary, on the other hand, walked on the rebellious side. One Saturday at lunch both boys came to our house.

When they came into the kitchen, one of my brothers had already left the table. Gary sat down and started eating what was left on his plate. My dad scolded him; if he was hungry he could have a new plate. Another time, one of my brothers had his BB gun out. Gary grabbed it and shot his own horse in the nose. The BB stuck and had to be pried out. Poor horse.

I guess Sue and Shorty reaped the financial rewards of all their show-business travel. They had a beautiful stone house on a small hill that overlooked a valley with a small river. All the rooms were done in knotty pine boards with matching doors. The rock fireplace that separated the living area from the kitchen area had a dual firebox. They'd carefully decorated the rooms in a Western motif. Old leather chaps hung on a wall in the living room, a worn-out saddle was thrown over a rugged-looking wooden horse in a corner, and Indian-type rugs covered the wood floors. My sister and her husband rented a second little house that sat on the Thompsons' property.

One year Shorty got the idea of planting strawberries on a piece of land close to the rental house. Unfortunately, that particular summer we experienced a shortage of rain. With a smaller-than-expected crop of berries, Shorty convinced Gary and Wayne, along with Lawrence, JE and me, to pick what berries existed.

We started picking, but it wasn't long before Wayne and I discovered arrowheads. At that moment, we lost all interest in berries. Our excitement with each flint discovery attracted the older ones' attention. Soon they too joined in the hunt. Naturally that led to throwing clods of hardened dirt at one another, which in turn led to trampling what poor berry plants remained as we ran around the field trying to avoid getting hit.

Word came back to us the next day that Shorty was not pleased about the lack of berries, not to mention his torn-up berry patch. I'm not sure whether Shorty punished Gary and Wayne, but I did notice he never replanted.

The Heads had three horses: Muskie, Queenie and Thunder. Muskie was a gentle, easy-to-ride Shetland pony. Queenie, though usually gentle, did like to sideswipe her rider against a fence on occasion. Then there was Thunder. Thunder resisted attempts to get close to him and intentionally upset Queenie if she got too far away. For safety's sake, our time with the horses was limited.

One day Gary rode Queenie to our house. While she was there, she decided she needed to let go of her bowels, which resulted in a pretty good-sized pile. Well, my brothers started telling Wayne and me how if you rubbed the manure in the right places you would grow hair. Of course we had to give this technique a whirl and couldn't wait for them to leave. They had barely gone down the road when we were well into rubbing the horse poop on our chest and, yes, even down our pants.

Boy, did it stink! And boy, did we realize in that moment that we were just fed some horse poop. Given the situation, we could only turn to our well pump to clean up—with little success. Plain water did not wash away the smell. I knew my mother was going to get to the bottom of this stink.

How old were we when we tried the hair-growing technique? Wayne wouldn't want me to say!

Growing up with performing parents must have rubbed off on Gary and Wayne. Later in life they both followed their parents into show business. Gary became a promoter for different acts. Wayne changed his name to Wayne Carson and became famous as a songwriter. He wrote "Always on My Mind," which Elvis recorded in 1972 and Willie Nelson made famous forever. Wayne loved telling how the song came to be: His wife was giving him the dickens for being gone for so long, so he told her over the phone that she was always on his mind, and at that very moment the words clicked. He quickly hung up, and that was the birth of a great song.

Strawberry picking aside, I worked quite hard as a youngster. I had one of the commonest jobs for budding employees: newspaper delivery. In the morning before school and in the afternoon after school, I delivered newspapers, regardless of the weather and regardless of Diz Stepp's bulldogs chasing me. I know there were only three, but I swear it seemed like three hundred!

I also had an uncommon job, though it was common in Walnut Grove: each fall I picked up black walnuts. Black walnuts and black walnut trees are often called "black gold." It takes fifty to eighty years before a sapling becomes most productive, rendering black walnut lumber a very expensive product. You could tell what boys (and on rare occasion a girl) had been picking up walnuts by the brown stains on their fingers. Walnut juice was impossible to wash off; it simply had to wear off. Our driveway was gravel, hard-packed with years of use. I would spread the walnuts up and down the driveway in the tire grooves. As my dad and others drove in and out, the pressure would eventually remove the hulls. Once the hulls were off I could sell the nuts to the Missouri Farmers Association, which then resold them. Some people, and not just kids, would put a good-size rock in the middle of the bag so when it was put on the scale they would get more money. I may have been mischievous at times, but I was not going to cheat. I had business integrity!

In fifth grade, I decided if I gathered up trinkets lying around the house, I could sell them at school to make some money. Each morning before the school bus arrived out front, I scrounged around the house for eye-catching items. With three older brothers, I had an almost endless supply of merchandise. Even at that age, I understood what it meant to ask for forgiveness rather than for permission; my brothers were never the wiser. At lunch-time, I would drag a desk out of the classroom into the hall and carefully lay out my trinkets for sale, each item carefully placed to show off its best side. Prices were a bargain, ranging from five cents to twenty-five cents.

I got a taste of entrepreneurship and I enjoyed every minute of it. I also enjoyed making several dollars each lunch period. But the thriving trinket business was about to meet with the authorities. The free market came under attack when one of the teachers, Mrs. Ethel Hagerman, decided to take democracy and freedom into her own hands and shut down a flourishing enterprise. She said, "Jonathan, pack up your stuff, put the desk back in the classroom, and don't do this again." When she said "stuff" I almost corrected her in defense of the free market: it was not "stuff"; it was "merchandise"! And, it was merchandise that freed people to live a life of luxury, which in my case meant consuming lots of candy and Bazooka bubblegum.

There was something about this experience that pointed me in the direction of business. I never forgot the simple thrill of using an idea to accumulate cash. Poor Mrs. Hagerman's name must appear in business books today as the person who stopped a young man from becoming the Sam Walton of Walnut Grove.

When I got old enough to start mowing lawns for money, I developed a new scheme: I would knock on doors to find new customers; other boys would mow the lawns and I would help them finish; then we'd share the fee, thus resulting in more money overall. Theoretically my idea was great, but in reality it wasn't practical. Growing the business made it hard to hold up my end of the deal to help them finish the lawns. Soon the other boys realized they were doing all the work while I rode around collecting money and finding customers. Turnover was high, and the talent pool was shallow. Dissension set in, and I was forced to declare the end of a great idea.

About the same time, I tried to drive a hay truck in the hayfields. I was only twelve years old (it was a different time!), so I had to sit on two empty Coke cases to get high enough to see out the windshield. I barely could reach the pedals, so when I tried to let out the clutch and give it gas, boy, did that thing buck. The hay would topple, and sometimes it threw a guy or two off the back. When it did, I could count to three, that truck door would swing open, and a huge hand would reach in and throw me to the ground. It wasn't long before they suggested I not come back.

But I wasn't to be kept down. I got on my bike and went from farmhouse to farmhouse asking the farmers if I could clean out the stalls in their barn for a quarter. In two days I learned two things: the first day I learned that manure is awfully heavy; the second day I learned I needed a lesson in wage pricing. The third day I put a Closed sign on the business.

By the time I reached junior high, I started teaching myself electronics. I picked up an Air Force electronics manual and started figuring out how to fix things. My dad bought me a tube tester, and I made resistor testers and capacitors that I checked with an ohmmeter, but mostly I would just guess how things worked. I dreamed my way to solutions. Folks in town began to bring me their radios and televisions for repair—which was a bargain because I charged only for parts. I had yet to learn what it meant to make a profit.

But even if cash was scarce, I was never afraid to ask for what I needed—or wanted. One day I needed a tri-square. I marched right down to the hardware store and asked to open a charge account so I could buy one.

"Does your mom know you're doing this?" asked Mr. Johnson.

"No," I said with no further explanation.

Well, my reputation amongst the townsfolk must've stood me in good stead. He shrugged. "OK."

Likewise when I developed a fondness for clothes and had a hankering for a new shirt, I went to the dry goods store. "Mr. Jones, I'd like to open up a charge account."

"Well," he said around the stogie in his mouth, "does your mama know about this?"

"No," I replied.

He looked at my 13-year-old self. "Well, OK. Go get yer shirt."

I paid them both off in a timely fashion, and continued to charge things occasionally. When there was something I wanted, I pursued it. When I had a dream, I took action to make it happen. And I continued to dream about success.

When you are poor, "success" almost inherently means "being rich." Our family rarely had anything new. For the eighteen years I lived at home, I remember my parents buying little new furniture: two chairs for the living room and one television. As a kid I slept in an army bed against the wall; I never had a big bed. But, I reminded myself, that small bed was more than a lot of people had.

I knew I didn't want to be a mail carrier or a teacher. And I didn't foresee law books or a stethoscope in my future. (Our doctor, cigar in hand, was not the picture of success for me.) I wasn't sure what path I would follow.

One day when I was about fourteen, I was riding my bike. As I came around the side of the house, a feeling suddenly swept over me and told me to stop. I did. What was this going on in my mind? Then it came to me, crystal clear: *One day you are going to have many successes.*

It was so real, and I couldn't dissect it because I didn't know what success was. But I received such a sense, such a powerful knowing that it was going to happen to me, that I never doubted it from that moment on: whatever I chose to do, I knew I would succeed.

We Climb the Ladders We Build

I was very shy when young, but as I grew older I overcame my shyness by acting out. In high school, I wasn't *real* bad; I just kept my name at the front of the teachers' and the principal's minds.

The most egregious thing I ever did was hit the principal, Mr. H. P. Edmonson, in the back of the head with half an orange. I could not believe how his hair fluffed out like a baby's fine hair. The bits of orange pulp and juice flew everywhere.

Mr. Edmonson did not see me, but he knew "It had to be Jonathan!" because my reputation preceded me. Mr. Edmonson threatened to whip me as he dragged me down the steps to the wood shop, but he was interrupted by a phone call and left me on the bleachers. Saved by the bell! When he was out of sight I decided to go home an hour early. I thought for sure my mom was going to learn of this little mix-up with the school officials, but nothing was ever mentioned.

I seemed to get caught up over matters that shouldn't concern me. One year I took shop, and each student had a locker for storing projects. The shop class got a new welding machine; instead of the old-fashioned acetylene torch, this was a new-fangled electric torch. Well, after a few lessons with the teacher I thought I was a pro—and an eager one to boot. One day I was the only one in the shop, so I decided to experiment with this intriguing piece of equipment. After all, I was a fifteen-year-old boy who experimented with everything! I rolled the machine over to the lockers and welded one of the hasps closed. Wow, what an exciting moment! It was so fun I decided to do the whole row.

The next day the lockers had to be chiseled open, and someone figured out I had done it. Boy, you would have thought I had committed a crime. I didn't see what the fuss what all about. My punishment was a lecture in the principal's office. It was quite painful, especially because I didn't know what was coming at the end. I couldn't believe they didn't tell my mother. I never understood how they figured out it was me—until I became a parent and acquired that same canny intuition.

I was restless. That's probably why I got in trouble so much. I had low grades and didn't much want to improve them. But I did dream a lot about life and how I fit into the world. I was always dreaming that one day I would become very successful. Not by anyone else's standards, but according to my dreams. During study hall, rather than studying, I spent time looking at the pictures in the *National Geographic* magazines. I found myself inspired. I wanted to travel to faraway places—to Africa or Russia or even just within the United States, as long as it was somewhere outside Missouri. And I knew one day I would own an art collection; I didn't know when or what it would be, but I loved looking at the *National Geographic* photographs.

Even back then I had the beginnings of a belief system about dreamers and non-dreamers: I shy away from people who don't dream; they add nothing to your future and in most cases they take you away from where you're meant to be.

New Year's Eve. Sixteen years old. After all those years of watching my brothers head out spiffed up with creased jeans and Brylcreem ("You're too little!"), it was finally my turn. My dad was at the VA hospital in Fayetteville, Arkansas, for one of his skin treatments, and my mom said I could stay out 'til the new year struck, so a buddy and I went cruising to a neighboring small town. We didn't do any drinking and, with limited funds, the evening consisted of little more than driving around listening to Elvis, the Platters and the Everly Brothers and admiring the cars of kids with money. I was partial to Cadillacs and Lincoln Continentals.

We returned to Walnut Grove around eleven and stopped at Lemon's service station, where the locals hung out late at night, to get a soda. When we walked in, one of the men—I don't remember who—said, "Jonathan, have you been home tonight?" I said "No," uneasy; something must be wrong for a question like that. He then said, "You'd better go home. I think your daddy died."

I was struck with fear and filled with panic. We jumped in my friend's car and he wasted no time in driving me home. Up the road far from my house, I saw the front porch light on and knew it was no rumor. My mom always left a table lamp on for me, but never the porch light.

When we pulled up to the house, JE's car was in the drive. He and his wife sat on the sofa in the living room, quiet and solemn. Without saying a word to them I headed to the kitchen to find my mom. We stood and hugged one another for a long time. I always worried about my mom; now I had even more reason to worry.

Later that night, the undertaker, who had just returned from the VA hospital with my dad's body, stopped by to drop off my dad's personal belongings. I was still in shock when he came into the room to speak to me. My father had died of a heart attack.

I sat there for the longest time just staring, running over and over in my mind what this meant. What was the last thing I had said to my father? I couldn't remember. What would be the effect on my mom? What was I supposed to do now? I dreaded the funeral. I dreaded being stared at. Losing my dad felt like a personal stigma. I felt set apart from the other kids. How would they act around me at school? What would they say?

The day of the funeral my mind still swirled with these new, strange feelings that I couldn't even define.

How could a sixteen-year-old pick them apart to find deeper understanding? I had lost a parent, a dramatic change in anyone's life.

The entire family came home for the funeral. My brothers had suits, but Mom had to borrow one for me. Over the years we often borrowed suits for school activities, and I never knew whose suit I was wearing. I never asked because I would have been too embarrassed to know, and now I had to wear a borrowed suit to my father's funeral.

It felt like half the town crammed into Brim's Funeral Home. People brought all kinds of food—more than hungry people could ever eat, and I had no appetite. I saw the faces of my schoolmates, and despite my feelings of unease, in a way it also made me feel good. They came in support of *me*, and I made it through the day.

With the funeral behind me, I returned to school. Some teachers and a few kids expressed their sympathy. I just wanted it to pass and be gone. I wanted to get to the "new normal," whatever that might be. At the same time a feeling crept in that made me feel guilty: relief. The gray cloud of my father's reticence and misery would no longer hang over our house. I would no longer need to feel embarrassed or ashamed by him. It's funny how some things seem so utterly consuming in the moment and lose meaning in hindsight.

What became critically important for my mother was money. My father had worked most of his adult life for the US Postal Service, so naturally my mother expected government death benefits and retirement income. My father hadn't told her he'd taken a higher salary in exchange for giving up his pension. She never got a thing. She went to work cleaning hotel rooms to support herself and me for as long as I was at home. Eventually, after I'd moved out, she sold the house and moved into a rental house. I wouldn't be in a position to help my mother for some time, but I promised myself when I had the chance I would buy her a house.

I was a troublemaker at times, but there was at least one class where I did not get into trouble: accounting. The class required that you keep a complete set of books including invoices, accounts receivable and accounts payable; at the end of each school week your books needed to balance. It felt surprisingly easy and natural to me, like breathing air. Accounting became one of my favorite classes, and somehow I knew it would serve me well in my future career, whatever that would be.

I also loved speech class. I loved being center stage.

When I was a young boy, I would gather my family in the living room and perform for them. I'd act like I was playing several parts in a play, or I would sing while strumming an old ukulele. They laughed and laughed, and I loved it. Later I realized that they were actually laughing at me, not my comedy, but I didn't care—I was having fun.

Mr. Jim Cummins, my speech teacher, did not laugh at me. On the contrary, students often regarded Mr. Cummins as too serious. I looked at it differently. I always thought he wanted the best from everyone, and, in time, he got it.

Mr. Cummins led the high school's participation in the Green County forensic speech contest. He encouraged me to participate and assigned me a Bible reading to recite, verses from Matthew and Mark. I still remember Matthew 6:19: "Do not lay up for yourselves treasures on earth...where thieves break in and steal." I won the county contest. Oh, what a rush! The thrill that came with the county victory got me through the disappointment of defeat at the state level.

A year later, Mr. Cummins directed the school play I was in. Too many years have passed to remember the name of the play, but I do recall I played "the father." My mother sat in the audience, and I looked forward to her comments afterward. I knew beforehand that she would offer a glowing review of my "night at the theater" (she was my mother, after all).

While I can't remember the details of the play itself, I remember vividly the feelings I experienced. During the performance I was calm and confident and, most important, I remembered all my lines! After the show, I felt exhilarated—full of growth and excitement and potential in this new love of speaking. A glowing review was well deserved.

Mr. Cummins taught me much about public speaking; I gained skills and knowledge I would use throughout my career. And he sparked the beginning of a dream in me—to speak before my high school alumni association.

Graduation day was a solemn day, or at least I thought I was supposed to think of it that way. In fact, even though I was filled with confidence and belief in myself and my future, I was still a bit scared. The time had come to swing out on the cable at Big Rock and let go at the right time, knowing that one mistake in timing could mean crashing into the rocks hidden below the water's surface.

I swung out and let go.

THE JOURNEY OF A THOUSAND MILES BEGINS WITH THE FIRST STEP

The day after I graduated from high school I got on a bus and headed to Santa Barbara, California. It was the first time I had ever been out of the state of Missouri. With all of twelve dollars in my pocket, I was determined to start fulfilling my dreams.

My mother had not interfered in my decision; I guess she recognized my choice as a rite of passage. She wished me well while holding back a few tears. Practically, my departure no doubt saved her money, but I know she worried about my being halfway across the country.

Across the street from the Santa Barbara bus depot was the YMCA. What luck. Things were working out already. I was scared but determined. I had made too many commitments to myself and to others to turn back now. If I went home I knew I'd only hear, "He couldn't make it." I would not let that happen.

I crossed the street to the Y and was told a bed cost twelve dollars for two weeks. After two days there, I realized the real YMCA had relocated two years before and this was now a dive joint. One morning an old guy, no doubt one of the winos, came into the community kitchen and proceeded to fry a can of Skippy's dog food for his breakfast. Now this small-town Missouri boy had never gone below rabbit or squirrel on the food chain (and I'm sure some folks would squirm over that) and didn't want to go any lower, but I was too broke to leave. I knew I had to find a job quickly—I did not tolerate hunger well and I refused to call home for money.

The first day of searching, I did not find a job. The second day I found a job washing dishes at night at Petrini's, an Italian restaurant in Santa Barbara. While working, all I could think about was break time so I could eat the free food they offered as "bonus" compensation. In the fall, I planned to start City College during the day and wash dishes at night. In the meantime, I found a day job upholstering caskets, but quickly ditched it when I found employment at United States Industry (USI), an electronics manufacturing plant in Goleta.

With my intense interest in electronics since my early teens, I thought I would major in electrical engineering, so USI suited me perfectly. I inspected missile parts manufactured for use on submarines. It didn't take me long to become a team leader overseeing a group of inspectors on the assembly line.

My good feelings about my success at USI were quickly dashed with an incident in the men's restroom.

Now, at our house we had Miss Hattie, our outdoor privy, but at Walnut Grove High School, we had a normal bathroom with a long trough urinal. For the full length of the urinal a water pipe very slowly dripped

24/7. (I imagine we drained the Lake of the Ozarks several times over the decades.) When I walked into the men's room at USI I was amazed by what I saw. Brown square tiles covered the floor and walls. The lighting was recessed into the ceiling and barely noticeable. The light level itself was dim, which reminded me of the chandelier in our living room when three of the five bulbs were burned out, but the resemblance ended there.

As I surveyed the room with awe, I noticed the most amazing urinal sitting right in the middle of the floor. All I could say was "Wow." I sure wished my brothers and friends back home could see this. The urinal was about four feet in diameter and eight inches deep with a sixteen-inch pedestal coming up in the middle and a bar that encircled the whole urinal near the floor. I thought to myself, *That's for flushing. Nice.*

As I was going to the bathroom in this wonderful invention the thought came to me, *Why would you want to stand here and do your thing with other guys across from you doing their thing?* I shrugged my shoulders and mumbled, "Well, that's California for you." When I finished, I looked for the sinks. At first I couldn't find them. *How different could they be?* I thought. I soon noticed that where I had just gone to the bathroom a man was washing his hands. I didn't know whether to laugh at my ignorance or turn red with embarrassment.

Did I quit because of this incident? Well, no, but I did feel relieved to start college in the fall.

As planned, I attended City College during the day and washed dishes at Petrini's at night. Within a few weeks I was moved from dishes to cooking. I liked this change: it meant more money and put me closer to the food for snacking. And the food was outstanding!

Petrini's was a family business, and I could see the bond was tight in the family. Three brothers, Geno, John, and Julio Petrini, owned the business. Mamma Petrini made the lasagna—several trays at a time, enough to last all week. "Pop" Petrini was short on words, but friendly and polite. He always dressed in coat and tie and reminded me of a gentleman from the "old country." The Petrinis were good honest people and hard workers. They started out in a small space; as business grew, they moved four doors up the street and kept the old location for cooking sauces and making raviolis. They were filled with family pride; I had to respect that about them.

The Petrinis offered me my first taste of good Italian food: they showed me how to make a real pizza. When I was sixteen my mom bought a pizza kit in a box, which included the dough, sauce and cheese. She unrolled the dough onto a cookie sheet, spread the sauce on it and topped it with the cheese. I could hardly wait for it to bake. Finally the time came. It tasted like the box it came in! She reminded me how fortunate I was to be fed pinto beans and fried potatoes on a regular basis. When I tasted real pizza for the first time at Petrini's, I was ready to convert.

All the food at Petrini's was prepared to the highest standards, no exceptions. But it wasn't just the food that kept the diners coming back. It was also the outstanding customer service, which was paramount to the way Geno, John and Julio ran the business.

First, they treated their employees with great respect. Training was a priority and no shortcuts were allowed. The Petrinis insisted, down to the smallest detail, that things be done right. For example, currency was to be put in the cash drawer face up with the faces on the bills pointed to the right.

Second, the Petrinis made every customer feel special, respected and appreciated. They greeted every customer coming through the door and thanked every customer on the way out the door. Something as basic as taking a customer's money could make that customer feel like royalty. The cashier carefully counted the change—each coin and each bill—into the customer's hands. Every customer also got a Tootsie Roll when they paid—simple and inexpensive, but very effective.

Petrini's did phenomenal business as a result of their guiding philosophy, and as time went by, I found myself becoming more and more interested in the food business. It's not that I didn't enjoy school, but as I sat in political science, literature and biology classes, my mind kept going back to my childhood dreams of success. School felt interminably slow. I needed to get on with my dreams, and the restaurant business might be the path to achieving my goals. At Petrini's each day I saw successful entrepreneurs who modeled my dreams. The sooner I got started, the sooner I would be able to join them. I never thought of myself as a quitter, but I found myself tempted to drop out of school.

One day at work John was sitting at the end of the counter. I told him how much I enjoyed the restaurant business and asked him if there was a chance for full-time employment. I could tell from his expression that he was giving the question his entire consideration. And then, standard for the brothers' partnership, he said, "Let me talk to Julio and Geno."

At nineteen, it was a tough decision, but I decided to join Petrini's full time. After the fact, I told my mom. She never tried to dictate how we should live our adult lives and, calm as always, said, "Honey, it's your choice and life. You need to make your own decisions."

Going to work full time wasn't the only big decision I made at the ripe old age of nineteen: I also decided to get married. Margie was a sweet girl I met during my brief stint at the casket upholstery shop. Her mother worked there with me, and Margie would pick her up after work. At nineteen, I was a grown-up, and getting married was what grown-ups did, right?

Margie and I started our marriage happily and within a few years had two children, a son and a daughter.

Soon after making the jump to full-time work, I began to run the small carryout unit in Goleta each Tuesday night while the Petrinis were off. This responsibility confirmed I would pursue the restaurant business as my future. My next break came shortly thereafter when Petrini's opened up a full-service store in Goleta and closed the carryout unit. At this new location, while I was not the official manager, I had a lot more managerial responsibility, and I loved it!

But loving my job didn't mean I didn't have a lot to learn. One early evening before the dinner rush, Julio said, "Hey, Jonny!" (He always called me Jonny and I liked that because I liked Julio.) "Go over to Jordano's and get me a pound cake."

I wanted to please Julio so I looked and I looked for this pound cake and finally I found a cake that matched Julio's request.

When I returned to the restaurant Julio said, "Jonny, what took you so long?"

"It took me a long time to find this cake," I said. With a bit of pride, I pulled from the bag a chocolate cake that weighed exactly a pound.

Julio's expression was a mixture of disbelief, surprise and maybe a bit of anger. He just turned around and went back to work. (I should note that I don't remember my mom ever baking a pound cake. She made either yellow cake with chocolate icing or chocolate cake with chocolate icing; during strawberry season, she baked angel food cake topped with strawberries and fresh whipped cream, likely from the cow that very morning.)

My pound cake fiasco must not have worried the Petrinis too much, because shortly after that little mix-up they made me general manager of their new restaurant in Santa Barbara.

This was the real test. I made sure I did everything by the book—their book. I ran a tight operation. I worked long hours and I demanded professional behavior from everyone. No loafing or goofing off. I was determined the customers would receive nothing but the best service. I was determined to do an outstanding job.

As a twenty-year-old manager, I was confronted with some real challenges in running the restaurant. One Friday night, the kitchen was slammed and I was helping the cooks get the food out in a timely manner. Earlier in the week, I had hired a new waitress (back then they were called *waitresses* rather than *food servers*), an older lady who seemed reliable. Suddenly I heard loud laughter coming from the dining room. I noticed our new waitress at a large table where the patrons—and those at the surrounding tables—were going bonkers. Apparently she could not find the plastic bibs that we tied on customers eating spaghetti. Instead, she was slipping toilet seat covers over the customers' heads! This was a test for cool, calm leadership. I was ready to take charge. Then I realized there was very little I could do to undo what was happening—and besides, the customers were enjoying the show.

As well as I performed as general manager, looking back, I realize how much more I could have done to build sales beyond quality food and great service. We rarely advertised or marketed in any intentional way; we just believed the product spoke for itself. And it did: people who knew of our location were loyal and visited us often.

While at Petrini's, I observed the world closely. I saw people dressed in something other than bib overalls. I saw celebrities on the streets of Santa Barbara. I started to see people with money and opportunity and freedom to do what they wanted, go where they wanted. I began to realize what fed my feelings as a kid. I started to be able to put those feelings into words. Success meant nice things and opportunity, and money was the measurement of success.

A gentleman named Miles Davis (not the famous musician) came in regularly. He was always decked out, dressed to the nines. One day he pulled off an alligator shoe to show Gino. "Got to go get a new pair of shoes. Starting to get a hole in the bottom," he said. I wanted to say, "I'll take them!" Well of course I didn't, but today I have several pairs of alligator shoes.

Each Saturday a group of businessmen came in for lunch, Carolos Bottiani, Italo Talevie and Jimmy Jordano among them. These names may bring *The Godfather* to mind, but all of them achieved great business success. For example, Jimmy Jordano and his brother, John, owned twelve large supermarkets, as well as wholesale companies that delivered produce, meat, liquor, beer and restaurant equipment to smaller markets and restaurants.

I wanted to be in a position to take a rightful seat at their table on Saturday mornings. I had a long way to go. I wondered what it would feel like—would it feel as grand as I imagined? Or would I have been just another guy pulling a chair up to the table—no big thing? As with the Petrinis, I had these gentlemen as role models and mentors, stars to shoot for. No one in Walnut Grove could inspire me like these businessmen did.

Another influential customer was Sam Battistone, Sr., cofounder of the 24-hour coffee-shop chain Sambo's. Sam Battistone, Sr., was a giant in the business world who for some reason took an interest in me. Imagine this young kid from Walnut Grove, Missouri, talking and associating with a man who started a restaurant chain that blanketed the United States! I knew his wisdom and business acumen were without competition.

He was calm and thoughtful as he spoke. He looked me straight in the eye, and he was all about business. Anytime we visited, I couldn't help but remember the amazing ability of my high school teachers and principal to sense my guilt for acts of mischief. I felt the same keen ability in Sam, and I suspected he saw me as an average manager.

Of course, I wanted to prove him wrong.

After a time, Sam began talking to me about the money that could be made with his company.

I knew what I must do.

When John came by the restaurant one morning, I told him with great sadness and regret that I was going to leave to work at Sambo's. But the Petrini family had established in my mind the standards by which I would judge every other restaurant. Forty-five years later, I still stay in touch with them.

The definition of success is different for each person. For some people it is achieving financial or business success; for others it is having a wonderful marriage. Unfortunately, marriage was not working out for me.

I realized it had been a mistake to think I was mature enough to get married at nineteen. I was just starting to explore the world and be out on my own at that age. As I discovered the possibilities around me, I realized I could not be the husband Margie wanted or deserved, and a poor marital relationship would not be good for our children. So, after deep thought and consideration, I decided that I did not want to stay in the relationship. I ended the marriage.

Shortly after Margie and I divorced, I started dating a woman I had hired as a waitress a few months earlier, Barbara. Within a year, we married. This time I thought it was for real.

THE DOOR TO SUCCESS IS LABELED "PUSH"

Sam Battistone and Newell ("Bo") Bohnett founded Sambo's in 1957. While the chain's name was created from a combination of the founders' names, Sambo's became associated with Little Black Sambo, so the chain used that theme in each location. Helen Bannerman's *The Story of Little Black Sambo*, originally published in 1899, tells the tale of an Indian boy who is chased by tigers and gives them pieces of clothing in exchange for not eating him. Jealous and vain, the tigers chase each other around a tree so fast that they turn into butter, which Little Black Sambo's mother uses to make pancakes. Hence, butter and pancakes, along with waffles, eggs and bacon, equaled a 24-hour coffee-shop chain. (Despite the story's being set in India, the Little Black Sambo image has become emblematic of "pickaninny" stereotypes about people of African background. While I am not going to dwell on this connotation, please don't think I am unaware of it.)

After joining Sambo's, my first restaurant was a low-volume store in El Centro, California, right in the middle of the Imperial Valley desert. How would I increase the sales volume? I decided my strategy had to be related to the staff.

The staff at the restaurant moved too slowly for my liking, didn't understand good service and didn't seem to be interested in getting any better. The applicants who came in to apply for jobs didn't have any quickness about them either; they lacked enthusiasm and fire. I was looking for upbeat, bubbly and cheerful, but for whatever reason—perhaps the 110-degree weather—the locals did not exhibit these traits. I knew I needed a different approach.

In the 1960s, a city's unemployment department was instrumental in placing people looking for work. With that in mind, I called the unemployment department in San Diego and got to know a wonderful lady, Marcia. I told her what type of waitress I had in mind: pleasant personality, prone to smile, energetic—and willing to move to the El Centro. In three months, I had replaced almost the entire waitress staff with these fine people from the coast of California.

The feeling and mood in the restaurant changed completely, both with the employees and the customers. The employees had fun and worked together well. Service became their number one goal, no exceptions! The restaurant was kept clean, with floors waxed and buffed weekly; everything glowed.

At the end of nine months, sales were up over thirty percent from the prior year and the store had made more money in that period than the prior two years combined.

I started with a store that had never made money; when I left, it had not only increased sales but was making a fifteen percent profit.

At Sambo's, numbers were the name of the game—increasing sales, managing food and labor costs and making a profit—and I loved it! Being able to compare myself to others was like throwing gas on a fire. It was an internal explosion of growth, knowing exactly where I had to build or improve. It was at Sambo's that I learned how competitive I really was, not only with others, but with myself. From the time I got up in the morning to the time I went to bed, the only thing I thought about was the numbers, always trying to outdo myself in all categories.

This was the springboard to the rest of my life. While I'd always felt it, during my time at Sambo's I learned that I really could accomplish almost anything I set my mind to. And in El Centro I realized I had a talent for turning around bad restaurants.

As a result of hard work with dedicated employees in El Centro, I got a call from the director of operations at Sambo's main office in Santa Barbara. In this chain of more than 500 restaurants he offered me a promotion to the highest-volume restaurant in the chain. No sales problem there! I told him I was ready to take that giant step out of the desert.

The restaurant was in Oakland, California, in Jack London Square, the popular entertainment and business district near the estuary that separates Oakland from San Francisco. Bars and restaurants lined the streets; Friday and Saturday nights were crazy with nightlife. I thought El Centro was tough, but this restaurant never slowed down. This one restaurant did over a million dollars a year in sales. So what, you say? Well, the average guest check was one dollar per person. A cup of coffee cost ten cents; for ten cents, a waitress still had to serve the customer and a dishwasher had to wash the cup and saucer and water glass. Think about how many people had to go through that business each day to produce sales in excess of one million dollars a year. At times, I was the highest paid busboy at Sambo's, but at the end of the year, I looked at my W-2 and smiled real big.

In some ways the pace of business was my smallest challenge. The outgoing manager, Dick Prado, was promoted to a position in Sambo's main office. Prado had a personality that made everyone like him from the get-go, and the employees absolutely *loved* him. He did a super job with this high-volume store. And yet right away, with my fresh set of eyes, I saw areas for improvement; I knew making some changes would increase profit immediately.

I was cautious not to rock the boat too soon; I didn't want a mass walkout. The employees were still loyal to Prado and the good money they were making under his leadership. He had trained them well, and they knew exactly what needed to be done—a completely different set of circumstances from what I had found in El Centro.

My gut told me the smartest way to approach this business was to leave the employees alone, keep restaurant operations on track, and focus on maximizing profit. Over the next few months, I did cut costs and increase profits, which of course made the main office officials happy, but I didn't mess with the employees or their work schedules. In my entire restaurant career, this was the only time I ever took a status quo approach with the employees, thanks to Dick Prado.

It's worth a brief description of Sambo's compensation structure, nicknamed "fraction of the action." In a nutshell, for every dollar of profit, fifty cents went to corporate, twenty cents went to the manager, who had to "buy in" on each restaurant he or she managed, and the remaining thirty cents went to other investors, including managers and supervisory employees who bought shares, or "pools." This unique arrangement gave managers and employees great incentive to work hard and increase profit. When stores functioned well, the camaraderie was great and the staff were upbeat and enthusiastic. As a manager I had quite a few fraction-of-the-action investments, and they brought me a nice income each month.

In 1972, while I was managing the Oakland store, Sambo's management decided to take the company public. Despite my management position, I did not have enough cash to invest. Yes, I had *some* cash, but I knew how big this IPO would be, and I wanted to take advantage of it on a larger scale. (Perhaps one might say I was greedy. Or tycoonish.) I remembered the lesson I'd learned early on: if you want something, ask for it.

Good restaurant managers recognize their regular customers and speak with them frequently. Nothing deep—just the typical chitchat with a smile, making sure the meal tastes good. One of the customers I spoke with on a daily basis was J. P. DeBernardi, an older gentleman who came in every morning. A waitress told me he was the owner of a highly profitable restaurant on the estuary, massive water rights, an electric company and more. In short, this man *did* have money.

Well, just like going to the hardware store and asking for a charge account, I went to Mr. DeBernardi's office with the idea of borrowing money. I walked in and introduced myself. (I didn't expect him to recognize me outside of Sambo's.)

"Have a seat," he said.

"Thank you, I'll stand," I replied. I knew that somewhere in the conversation I had to keep an upper hand. I proceeded with my request to borrow money in order to invest in Sambo's IPO. I told him I would pay him back and split the profit with him.

I got the same look from him than I did from the man at the hardware store when I was a teenager.

"Come with me," he said.

I followed him downstairs to his blue Cadillac. He opened the trunk. The only thing in it was a black briefcase with white stitching. He took out one of those big checkbooks that has three checks on a page. He wrote a check, handed it to me, and said, "Good luck."

The check was for fifty thousand dollars.

Sambo's went public, the stock soared, and in six months I had paid Mr. DeBernardi back his fifty thousand dollars plus another fifty thousand in profit, and I still put fifty thousand in my own pocket.

By the early 1970s I was earning over $125,000 a year, which would be in the neighborhood of a half million dollars annually today. I was also working seventy or eighty hours a week and never took a vacation. How could I say no to making such sums of money? While the money was good and it allowed me the opportunity to do many things, including buying my mother a new house, it did keep me away from Barbara and our young son.

After a couple of years in Jack London Square, I was promoted to district manager in Montana. When this promotion came about, I saw the opportunity to do well and advance my knowledge and career. I was excited by the idea of having more time to spend with my family, which grew to include a daughter while we were in Montana, but I quickly learned I had miscalculated the geographical layout: covering all of Montana and the northern part of Idaho required out-of-town travel for several days each week.

Nonetheless I went about the job determined to make big improvements in the two regions. At that time, the entire state of Montana had a population of around nine hundred thousand people, so, as you can imagine, increasing sales was a real challenge. It required the stores to operate at maximum levels, especially in service. I incorporated the same methods I had used in El Centro. We raised the hiring standards: we looked for waitresses who had a great smile, a bubbly personality and a desire to serve the customer. This method, while it worked, was slow in implementation and required monthly progress evaluations with the managers. They had to make a concerted effort to hire a good waitress, fire the lowest-ranked waitress, and then repeat the process. Several managers understood the reasoning but lacked the courage to rid the operation of the weakest link in the chain.

Marketing dollars were scant at best. We focused on local community involvement to gain recognition and help draw more customers to the stores. The great distance from one store to the next rendered cooperative marketing ineffective. The miles were long, with nothing in between; I started recognizing the antelopes as I flew by. *Beep-beep!* I honked.

I directed my efforts at increasing profit, an area that could show some immediate progress (very much like the strategy I had used at the Jack London store). By the end of my seven years in Montana, all the numbers showed remarkable gains. All in all, it was a successful assignment, but the time to move on was getting closer.

By 1977 Sambo's had grown to more than 1,100 restaurants, and was now run by Sam Battistone, Jr., the cofounder's son. I continued to invest in Sambo's around the country. But a funny thing happens when a company goes public: the investors want to make sure they get a return on their investment. Over the next few years, investors got frustrated that fifty percent of profits went to managers and other owners, so Sam Battistone, Jr., decided to change the compensation program to satisfy the stockholders. When he took away the "fraction of the action," managers' and supervisors' financial incentive to work so hard evaporated. *Poof.* Managers questioned this and other corporate decisions, leading hundreds of them to walk out. On top of the financial upheaval, by the 1970s the imagery of Little Black Sambo was drawing stronger and stronger criticism for its racial overtones, causing the company to begin renaming restaurants. By 1982 most of the restaurants would be sold, and Sambo's would go out of business.

By about 1977, even before the chain went out of business, I had lost most of my investment in Sambo's. The many shares of stock I owned became worthless. All the buy-ins for my management portions and the additional shares I had purchased had lost their value. To make all these purchases (as well as other investments, such as real estate), I had taken loans. At the time, the return on the investments had far exceeded the loan interest, making this a smart approach, but when all the Sambo's income dried up, I found myself deep in debt and unable to make payments.

I had three options: declare bankruptcy, liquidate my assets—all the real estate, stocks and other investments I'd been carefully building—to pay off my debt, or make a career change to increase cash flow so I could make the payments.

Bankruptcy was out of the question, partly because bankruptcy had a much greater negative impact then than it does now, but more so because I couldn't have lived with myself. My word was even more important to me than a legal contract, and I was not about to break my word to any of my creditors. I also didn't want to liquidate all my assets—that would take me backward financially, putting me back at square one.

It was time to make a big career change.

TO STRIVE, TO SEEK, TO FIND, AND NOT TO YIELD

Around 1977, when things were getting tough for me, the Golden Corral restaurant chain was getting established. The founders saw Sambo's successful results and were intrigued. They interviewed Battistone and Bonnett, and then structured the Golden Corral management compensation in almost the same way Sambo's initially had, with a 20% buy-in and share to the manager, and the option to purchase additional investment "groups" of 5% of the profit from a set of restaurants.

As Sambo's began its decline, many of its employees, myself included, migrated to the East Coast to join Golden Corral. With our experience during the peak profitability years at Sambo's, we had a lot of knowledge to contribute. We knew how to build sales, increase profit and recruit good managers. I began buying 5% groups as quickly as I could; as the company grew, the groups began to give me a hefty return. With my regular salary, my management bonus, and my groups, I was able to pay off all my debt. It wasn't easy, though.

My wife, Barbara, supported my decision to climb out of this financial hole rather than file for bankruptcy or divest of assets, and her stoic attitude helped us make it through this laborious ascent. One winter day, we ran out of fuel oil for heat. Thank goodness for the fireplace. I searched all around the property for any kind of wood to burn—in the garage, behind the garage, every place imaginable. We needed two days' worth of fuel until the next check arrived. My wife never complained, and we managed to stay warm with the bits and pieces of wood I scrounged up.

Another debt-related incident rocked my foundation. Golden Corral had just opened a new restaurant and one of the co-owners of the company was on hand for the big event. When he was ready to fly home, he asked me to take him to the airport. He wanted to ride in my Jaguar X12. What I hadn't mentioned to him was that the car was up for sale because I could no longer afford it. I didn't even have enough gas in the car to take him to the airport and get myself home—*and I didn't have enough money to buy any more gas.* How could I dissuade him without revealing my embarrassment? What would he think of having someone who couldn't even afford to buy gas running his restaurants and managing millions of dollars? My record spoke for itself, but sometimes facts are not enough to overcome impressions. I felt tense and awkward. I don't remember how I talked him out of a ride, but I kept my personal dilemma to myself—or at least I think I did.

The pressure started getting to me. I felt pressure to make financial targets so I would get promotions and bonuses. I felt pressure at home; though my wife was supportive, the situation took a toll on her and our children. I felt pressure to maintain the appearance of success despite our debt, which I attribute partly to ego and partly to legitimate concern about my business image. It was a tough row to hoe.

Today I would still make the same choice: to not sell assets, to not file for bankruptcy. My theme song then was Frank Sinatra's song "I Did It My Way." But after the experience of climbing out of debt, I determined never to get ahead of myself again. Any investments I made from then on would be with cash, not loans.

Today most people know Golden Corral for the namesake buffet-style restaurants, but while I worked there the corporation also owned several subsidiaries, including Carolina Chicken (the holding company for Church's Chicken), a chain of rib joints, a small Mexican restaurant chain, some oil-change shops and some budget hotels. Each of these businesses had its own president; all the presidents reported to the same board of directors. In 1986, I was named president of Carolina Chicken, and oversaw Church's Chicken and the Mexican chain.

Not surprisingly, Golden Corral eventually made a decision similar to Sambo's about the compensation structure: they wanted to purchase all the "groups" back to keep the profit in the corporation. Well, I'd been through that situation before and knew what could happen. I immediately accepted the offer: Send me a check, I said, and you can have my shares back. Though the glorious financial returns were over, I was (and continue to be) grateful to all the owners, leaders and friends at Golden Corral for the opportunity to recover and to prosper.

In the late 1980s, I attended a seminar with Victor Kiam as the speaker; he had just written his best-selling book *Going for It!: How to Succeed as an Entrepreneur*. Readers of a certain age may remember Kiam from the Remington electric shaver commercials in the late 1970s and 1980s: "I was so impressed, I bought the company!" (He also owned the New England Patriots for many years.)

I believe in the saying, "Go for it!" I also believe that life, if lived authentically, falls into place, and patience is an important part of the prescription. We're often too self-absorbed to notice opportunities; sometimes we need a strong push to find dreams that are right in front of us. Golden Corral offered me the opportunity to fulfill one of my lifelong dreams: owning my own business.

In the late 1980s the marketplace began to shift and become more challenging for a variety of reasons. Golden Corral decided to focus on its core flagship restaurants and divest of all the smaller subsidiaries. I was in a Victor Kiam situation: I knew the Church's Chicken chain (I'd overseen it, after all), I liked it and I wanted to buy it. I bought ten restaurants.

When the sale was finalized, I immediately went to work on my plans to address the new market challenges, build sales and increase profit. My sales strategy was simple: customers needed to feel like they got more than they paid for. In this type of restaurant business, we relied on customers coming back two and three times each week. Eighty percent of our revenue came from twenty percent of our customer base. We had to offer them value, value and value!

To improve profit, I chose economical ways of running the corporate office: I found small, inexpensive office space; I bought used office furniture; I had only one phone line installed; I found the smallest, cheapest copier that would get the job done; I negotiated with the payroll company for a lower price by doing some of the work in-house. My goal was to keep corporate costs down, as low as I could get them.

I loved the added responsibility of owning my own company. I had hundreds of employees in my eleven stores, but there was no one to turn to in case of a problem. It was all on me. Rather than letting it scare me, it made me more determined to succeed. I loved it because it made me stronger.

Buying a restaurant business with confidence felt easy to me; after all, I had turned around whole regions on several occasions with different companies. I used common sense to solve problems and encouraged people to do things right the first time. This approach made things easier and more manageable. The employees worked within well-established boundaries, but even with clear guidelines and expectations they had the opportunity to be creative. I recognized quality staff, and I let them do what they were hired to do in the first place. I offered my employees total honesty and didn't promise what I couldn't deliver; I'd seen too many leaders make promises I knew they would never fulfill. My *yeses* meant yes and my *nos* meant no. I didn't want to *look* like a good guy; I wanted to *be* a good leader, and I believe my employees were happy with my leadership.

My time at Golden Corral and Church's Chicken was not without its lessons. But this time the lessons were not about hiring good staff or managing profitability—that was the easy stuff. This time the lessons were personal.

The morning of my forty-fourth birthday, as I got dressed to attend a board meeting, I began experiencing discomfort from indigestion. I was in my teenage son's room complaining about it. He looked at me for a moment, then picked up the phone and dialed the family doctor, who directed me to go to the emergency room immediately. I was having a heart attack.

The news was not good: at age forty-four, I had heart disease.

After being put on medications and released with a strict diet protocol, I went to work on the mental shock of the news. I felt old, used up. I felt like my career was over, like I would not be taken seriously any more.

I lost weight and exercised every day. I stopped smoking. My last cigarette was the one I'd puffed as my wife drove me to the emergency room; I thought if my trouble was heart related I'd best have one more for the road, as the saying goes.

This was the first time I felt like I'd hit a wall in life that I couldn't fix.

While I continued to deal with my heart attack and the resulting necessary lifestyle changes, I could sense my marriage was not going well. Little could be done to change my years of absence, my not being a full-time partner. I enjoyed business, I got a thrill from working, and I worked too much. My wife and I had grown apart.

I did not want my marriage to come to an end. I did not want my family to fall apart. I told Barbara I would do anything to hold our marriage together; she could do anything she wanted.

It didn't help.

The pressure was almost unbearable. I felt a huge burden with my poor health and my marriage failing. I wondered what more could go wrong. I didn't have to wait long.

The Iraqi invasion of Kuwait, the Gulf War, Operation Desert Storm—these events caused uncertainty about the future throughout the US. When there is uncertainty about the future, consumers become cautious and slow their spending. Customers who used to come in to our restaurant two or three times a week slowed to once a week or once every two weeks. I began to hear customers wonder, "Will I be employed next week?"

The entire economy took a dive. Sales dropped by twenty percent in the restaurants I had just bought. I could no longer make the necessary payments to the lender and franchisor.

I became very angry at God. I looked forward to walking the dogs in the late evening so I could curse God out loud, and yes, I did curse God, unlike Job, who suffered far more than I did and would not curse his Creator.

I sometimes woke up very early, at three or four in the morning, a sign of depression. I remember one early morning I just lay there looking out the window. The sky had a blue tint that silhouetted the bare tree right outside the window. It was a depressing sight, eerie and cold, and the early hour only added to the awful mood. I felt like my life was over.

But I'm not a quitter. Three big crises had hit me— health, marriage and business—and there was only one I could repair or make go away: the business. This just happened to be the area that I felt most comfortable with, so I dug in deeper to fix it.

Try as I might, the business continued to head for bankruptcy, and my willpower dwindled. My attorney suggested we visit a lawyer who dealt in bankruptcy cases. As I sat and listened, I became more and more convinced that bankruptcy was not for me. When we returned to the car I turned to my attorney and said, "You and my accountant need to get together with my lender and franchisor and work out a plan that meets everyone's needs, because I'm not filing for bankruptcy!"

Regardless of the economic outlook, I took my stand. My firmness of position along with my plan to improve the current circumstances convinced my attorney and accountant to go along with me.

However, I was still relying completely on myself. I knew I needed someone stronger, and I knew who that was. Before I immersed myself in what was ahead, I got on my knees and turned the business and myself over to the Lord. While the words had passed my lips as a ten-year-old boy, they sank into my heart as a grown man.

The change was undeniable: suddenly, I started dealing with all three crises more comfortably and more effectively.

I saw some new angles to marketing and pricing that I hadn't thought of before. As often happens in such cases, the changes resonated with the customers and the business started to grow. I hired three teenagers to paint the exterior of the buildings. We added extra help before it was needed; I believed we had to look like we were still in business. I hired Troy Reaves, a natural restaurateur who would later become my director of operations.

As I told my attorney and accountant, I was determined not to go down Sambo's path of leaving lenders in the dust. Within a year I honored every single debt I had; not one went unpaid. While I closed my least profitable restaurant, overall sales and profit increased so much that I acquired four more restaurants. Cash flow continued to increase, and the bank accounts grew beyond belief. I knew why, and it wasn't me. It was my new CEO, God. For the next ten years, we never had a down year in sales.

Unfortunately God didn't fix everything.

My wife proceeded to file for divorce. I take most of the responsibility for the relationship's failure, but it doesn't matter who said what or who did what; the marriage was over, and I was devastated. The divorce got underway and ended as most do, with each party settling for a compromise on what he or she wanted. Though the children were out of school, I worried that the divorce was especially tough on them.

And in spite of dedicated dieting and physical activity, over the next several years I had three more heart attacks. Even so, I became stronger with each storm in my life and I learned to handle them with peace and a calm spirit.

In February 1995, at the end of my trifecta of crises, my mother passed away. Throughout this difficult period, I'd kept the worst from her. As she aged she'd eventually had to move from the beloved little house I'd bought her into a nursing home. After spending her entire life being independent, her heart must have been broken by this change. I didn't want to break it further, and nothing would have been gained by burdening her with my trials. But she retained that uncanny parental intuition, and in her later years she would ask me from time to time if everything was OK.

My mother made all the necessary arrangements for her funeral, even down to the preacher who would conduct the service. The only thing I had to do was write her obituary. At the memorial, the room was packed with people wanting to pay their respects: friends and neighbors from Walnut Grove and Springfield, but mostly her children, grandchildren and great-grandchildren. She was buried next to her adoptive parents at a cemetery in Republic, Missouri.

The family mainstay was gone. The matriarch so loved by all the family members would never again offer her common sense or help heal shattered dreams. My mother never took sides; she never caused division in the family. She never wavered from her loving, giving self. She always sent me a check for ten dollars on my birthday and for twenty-five at Christmas, none of which I cashed. She never stopped being "Mom." What a wonderful testimony to honestly say not one negative word was ever uttered about her.

When I was a child, I would often pray to God to take me before my mother. I figured my dying first would be easier on her than her dying would be on me. Later in life I came to realize this wish was based on my childhood fears of abandonment; my mother would have been devastated to lose one of her children and would have suffered for the rest of her life.

For her sake, I'm glad that God didn't answer those prayers, but I sure do miss her.

KNOWLEDGE IS THE WISDOM
OF ALL GOOD THINGS

With God as my CEO, business at Church's Chicken flourished, and with increased cash on hand, I started putting together my plans to enjoy the fruits of my labor and the blessings I'd received. I was a dreamer, and it was time to make some of my dreams come true.

I started my first art collection.

Naturally, I preferred a religious genre. I loved the stories of the Bible painted on canvas. Fine brushstrokes delicately captured the solemn mood and facial expressions of Christ praying in the garden, the Three Wise Men pondering the future and frightened Joseph fleeing the grip of Potiphar's wife.

I was hooked.

When you become a collector your initial impulse is to acquire, acquire, acquire, but it's not long before you sense something is lacking. My friend and art dealer, Robert Mayo, and his wife, Margaret, who introduced me to the world of buying art, pointed out the significance of research—the fun in collecting comes with knowledge of the items. Learning *who, what, when* and *where* broadens the enjoyment and intrigue of collecting. *Who* created the object that you've collected? *What* are the components of the piece? *When* was it created? *Where* was it created? Answering each of these questions can be as in depth as you want the research to take you. The more you know about the artist, the more intimate you become with your collection. Once I developed the research habit, I enjoyed collecting so much more; I couldn't believe how much breadth and depth it added to what I already loved.

As my knowledge of different art genres grew, I knew I wanted to change the direction of my collection. My collection of religious art held a very deep and personal connection for me, and I had mixed emotions about selling and donating the pieces. I enjoyed and I wanted others to enjoy this beautiful work, but I also wanted to expand my repertoire. I kept one wonderful watercolor of a seated Christ surrounded by Roman soldiers, and I began to consider my next move.

Religious art can be difficult to locate, but regional art can easily be found across the country. One particularly well-known area is Bucks County, Pennsylvania, part of the Delaware Valley. Many artists there trained at the famous Pennsylvania Academy of the Fine Arts. This area became my new focus.

With regional art you can quickly stick out your hand and grab something, but it is better to study the artists who appeal to you and then patiently wait for the right piece to come along. This process takes time; however, with my level of intensity, I put together a very nice collection in two years.

I slowly realized, however, this was still not the right collection. There was no unity: it lacked direction, it lacked purpose and it lacked depth and breadth.

An art friend, William Chaney, and I one day discussed what to look for in selecting a piece of art to buy. William said, "Always buy art you like."

I said, "There has to be more to it than that. I agree on that one point, but it must fit within the parameters of the collection."

He said, "Yes, but first and foremost, you have to feel like it is your best piece collected so far; if you don't, you will grow to hate it."

After some reflection on that last point, I understood what he meant. I had to keep reminding myself not to rush in putting together what I hoped would be a great collection and thereby miss the real importance of owning art. Quality stands out in all things—whether it's show dogs or new cars or Kentucky thoroughbreds. When something is really stunning, your eye will know it—and you'd better be ready to pay for it. (There is a balance between what you like and what you're willing to pay. Nonetheless, don't avoid being a collector simply because of price; I know people with very inexpensive collecting habits who wouldn't part with a single item in their collection.)

Around then, my dear friend Robert Mayo told me about a North Carolina artist who painted mostly in the Tryon area. *Here I go again*, I said to myself.

I began my research and almost immediately I knew this collection of North Carolina art would be my last collection—and I knew it would give me great satisfaction.

About an hour from Asheville, North Carolina, Tryon is a tiny town in the Blue Ridge Mountains that boasts a thriving arts community, many horse farms and a moderate climate. Half the people living there are transplants, presumably attracted by Tryon's many virtues. Tryon is also known as a place where you can find some of the best North Carolina mountain art, with pieces dating back to the early 1900s. Nowell Guffey, owner of Foothills Fine Art, has made it possible for me to have some of the finest works in my collection—not only paintings, but also carvings, pottery, baskets and quilts. Nowell has become a good friend over the years; we can spend hours talking about the Blue Ridge Mountains and the people who live there.

My North Carolina collection has two major components: a traditional collection from the nineteenth and twentieth centuries, and a contemporary collection. The highest honor that can be paid to an art collector is for a show to be dedicated to his or her collection. I am tickled to say that my North Carolina collection has received great recognition and has been exhibited in several museums on the East Coast.

The Longwood Center for the Visual Arts, part of Longwood University in Farmville, Virginia, exhibited my collection for several months. The art director, K. Johnson Bowles, did a fabulous job hanging the seventy-nine pieces of art throughout the gallery. One wall displayed the name of the exhibition, *Scent of the Pine, You Know How I Feel,* in large letters with my name in smaller letters underneath. The name came from the pine trees in the North Carolina mountains and the song "Feeling Good," famously sung by Nina Simone.

> *Stars when you shine, you know how I feel.*
> *Scent of the pine, you know how I feel.*
> *Oh, freedom is mine, and I'm feelin' good.*
> *It's a new dawn, it's a new day, it's a new life for me,*
>
> *And I'm feelin'...good.*

When I saw the wall I thought, *This kid from Possum Trot had no idea he would grow up to experience such a great honor and accomplishment.*

The catalogue, which contained all the images of the exhibition and a biography of each artist, was finely crafted—a work of art itself. (Later, I even saw a catalogue for sale on eBay.) On the front cover was a painting by Constance Cochrane titled *In Clouds on Grandfather Mountain* from around 1917. The scene is atop Grandfather Mountain, focused on a pine tree on a rock outcropping with low clouds framing the top of the painting; in the background you can see the rolling Blue Ridge Mountains. Cochrane was a much-respected artist who studied and exhibited at the Pennsylvania Academy of the Fine Arts; her paintings are difficult to find and in high demand. *Grandfather Mountain* suited the *Scent of the Pine* theme perfectly.

Opening night was beyond my imagination. I enjoyed answering questions from the visitors and sharing points of interest that were not commonly known about either the artists or the paintings. (In hindsight, I wish I'd spent more time with the interested viewers and less with the formal dignitaries!) My immediate family attended with me; I only wish my parents and siblings could have been there as well.

Critic and author Kim Herzinger states that collecting is a means by which one relieves a basic sense of incompletion brought on by unfulfilled childhood needs. When I read that I almost stopped collecting. While I agree with the notion that collecting can bring the past to the present, I couldn't square the idea of "incompletion" with my life. I think people who collect are trying to capture history or remember the past. I continue to collect everything from art to first-edition books to silver cigarette lighters, and I love the fact that each of my collections speaks of who I am and what I'm about.

In a follow-up conversation with my good art friend William Chaney, I deliberately guided our discussion back to the selection of art one loves, because I wanted to make a confession. "William," I said, "I agree with you totally about liking what you buy. I love every piece of art in my North Carolina collection. I love when I walk by the pieces; I just look at each one and smile! I'm that pleased with everything."

William asked, "Do you feel that way about all of the other items that you collect?"

My answer: "YES."

My business continued to grow steadily. I owned thirteen restaurants by this time, and began turning more and more of the daily operations over to Troy and the other great people who worked for me. I had learned that people do pretty well if you leave them alone, and I felt good leaving my people alone.

This financial success and confidence in my staff allowed me the opportunity for another great adventure — or maybe I should say another giant learning curve and the fulfillment of a past desire. I had never stopped regretting the fact that I had dropped out of college, and this was my chance to reverse that regret. But with so many fine schools in the region, which school should I attend?

Even though I had accepted Jesus, I still had a lot of doubt, as many people of faith do. Perhaps I could use this as an opportunity to learn about religion as well as to get a degree. In 1995, to test the waters, I signed up for a summer class at Southeastern Baptist Theological Seminary in Wake Forest, North Carolina.

I fell in love with everything about the campus. The professors were not only genuine but nice, and I could tell the students attended because of their love for the

Lord. This was where I wanted to be. I wanted to go to seminary. But it wasn't that easy.

Southern Baptists have strong objections to divorce, and I'd been through two. My application for admission was denied. No way was I giving up that easily. I visited the dean of students and stated my case: "I want to go to school here because I want to learn about God, my CEO." "Well, OK," he finally replied.

While I got my request, my entrance into school came with caveats. I was told more than once—with stern stares—that they would not recommend me for the pulpit, not even in a classroom. Did I wish they didn't feel that way about me? Yes; it hurt. But though I wanted to be called to the pulpit, I never actually felt the call. Apparently that wasn't God's plan for me, and God doesn't make mistakes. He knows a guy like me shouldn't be in the pulpit.

Seminary was one of the best times of my life; I loved being on campus with the professors and students. My classmates were not your typical 20-something poor college students. Many were older and had given up high-paying jobs, nice homes and comfortable lifestyles to return to school; their families came with them. I was still running my multimillion dollar business with more than 300 employees. I had wonderful staff at Church's, but I couldn't abdicate. I oversaw operations while taking a full load of classes. My days started at 6:30 in the morning and didn't end until 11:30 each night. I did this seven days a week for four years. I loved it.

A couple of years in, at the start of a semester, a new professor asked the students to tell him a little about themselves and what they had given up in order to attend seminary. By this time the students were well aware that I was in the restaurant business, so my answers had become rather abbreviated. When asked by the professor what I did, I replied, "I have thirteen Church's." He jumped back a bit and said, "Who are you—God?" Everyone got a big laugh out of this, and I explained to him the real meaning of Church's. (Of course, *he* then proceeded to explain to *me* the real meaning of *churches*.)

My unusual position outside school offered me some personal benefits at school. On more than one occasion I had the great pleasure of dining with the president, Dr. Paige Patterson, and his wife, Dr. Dorothy Patterson, at their home. Their son, Armore, made it possible for me to go to Zimbabwe on a hunting safari, a childhood dream come true.

I traveled to Kenya on a mission trip and then met Armore in Harare, Zimbabwe. We spent four days in this wonderful land; it was like a fairy tale. The locals dressed in their customary garb. I was awestruck to see wild animals out in the open, roaming around; a person really had to pay attention to the surroundings with the possibility of an animal lurking in the brush or around the next corner. I did get my trophy: a zebra rug is on my living room floor as a reminder of this trip. The whole experience far exceeded what a kid from Walnut Grove could ever have imagined.

My greatest pleasure was in giving back to God, who lifted me up and out of my despair. I paid for many students' tuition, books and housing at Southeastern. After Hurricane Fran passed through the greater Raleigh area in 1996, for many days the Southeastern cafeteria was the only building in the area that still had power. I arranged to have the cafeteria set up to feed all the students and their families until the extreme flooding receded and power came back on. God works things out; He put me in the right place at the right time to help.

My next great thrill came in making donations for students to go on mission trips. I had been on mission trips myself and knew the sense of fulfillment I found in reaching out and helping others, and I wanted to fund students who otherwise could not afford to go. I made all these donations anonymously; I knew other students had given up a lot to be in seminary, and I wanted to help without making them feel uncomfortable.

In December 1999 I graduated with an undergraduate degree in biblical studies. I'll never forget when I walked across the stage, received my diploma and shook the hand of the president, Dr. Patterson. I had become the only one of my siblings to finish college. While I had looked forward to graduation, I was sad as well, because I would no longer be in this fantastic learning environment. I made many friends at seminary, some of whom I'm still in touch with. The campus, the professors, the students and the learning all would be missed. I considered going into the master's program, but after four years, I was tired and needed to turn more attention to the business. So, I said goodbye to a fabulous time in my life—an experience that offered me a rebirth in a way. But I would never truly leave…

Today I sit on Southeastern's Board of Visitors, and I continue to contribute to my alma mater financially (one donation funded the All Library Catalog Of Theological Treatise—ALCOTT!). And the person who rejected my application initially? We are the best of friends today and I am supporting his mission, a seminary in El Salvador. Isn't it divine how those things work out? My experience at Southeastern made me realize that my religious mission was indeed not in the pulpit. My mission was to do good things with God's money.

I gave a lot of money to God and the church, but I treated myself generously as well. I bought a house at the beach and a house in the mountains. I traveled regularly to my vacation homes and around the world. I've explored nearly thirty countries—mostly by myself. Many people prefer to travel with a spouse or friend, but I was content on my own. Perhaps all that time as the youngest child, dreaming under a tree, taught me to be alone with myself. And now that I had grown up, I could make those dreams of adventure come true.

One of my most memorable trips was to Russia, the country I feared as a kid after all the grade school drills of ducking under our desks. I still harbored apprehension when the plane landed in Moscow, but I was too excited to worry about bombs and air raid drills. Once I was in the airport, I just stood and looked all around trying to figure out this strange place and the emotions I was feeling. The people were different: they dressed in heavy winter clothes, never looked anyone in the eye and were very quiet. Was this due to the influence of the Kremlin? Did they behave this way so they wouldn't stand out? I spent three days in Moscow sightseeing. Red Square was impressive with its huge expanse of red brick paving, St. Basil's Cathedral at one end and Lenin's tomb at the other, and I took some beautiful photographs of old Greek Orthodox Churches.

Sometimes I went a little too far in my indulgence in the good life. For a couple of years I had a thing for flying to various places just to eat, stay overnight and come back the next day. In New York, it was a French bistro; in Laguna Beach it was Javiers's; in Montana, Eddie's Supper Club; in North Carolina, the Grove Park Inn. While collecting Bucks County art, I often visited Philadelphia and spent time at my favorite art auction house. I usually stayed at the Four Seasons and ate at the famous Fountain Restaurant. Sometimes I'd take the first-class morning train to New York with all the DC dignitaries; after a day of seeing the sights, I could catch the five o'clock train back to Philly. I ate some of my best steak dinners ever on that train.

One of my favorite jaunts was Las Vegas. I loved the Bellagio. Now as you might imagine, gambling is not my cup of tea. I worked hard for my financial success and while I might be willing to gamble on myself and my business, I couldn't imagine risking money on pure chance. Losing a mere $200 would make me sick for days! So I am not exactly Vegas's target customer.

On one trip I met the grandson of the gentleman who started a well-known window company. He mentioned that the Bellagio had sent a driver to pick him up at the airport. Well of course I wondered why they weren't sending a driver to pick *me* up! One of the pit bosses explained, "You have to gamble for us to chauffeur you around." *Ah*, I thought, *I guess I will take taxis since I'm not a gambler and don't want to be a gambler.* But I'd made a connection with this pit boss, and after that I had an "in" for some of best shows Vegas had to offer: Jerry Seinfeld, Jay Leno, all the big names. All I had to do was call up this guy and let him know when I was coming and he'd get me front row seats. I tipped him amply, and it was worth it to me.

Can you imagine? This snot-nose kid from Walnut Grove, Missouri, who rarely got to go out to eat and had barely enough money to pay for a 15-cent hamburger when he did. All this travel, all this fine food, all this entertainment. Oh, my excitement and delight! I couldn't believe my good fortune. The kid who used to sit under the maple tree dreaming had made his dreams come true. It is a scary thing to say that you ended up in life with what you wished for.

I often made dinner reservations at the Bellagio's Prime Steakhouse. I knew the maître d' and I always requested a specific table and a specific waiter. The first time I was seated at Table 4 (as a restaurateur, I knew to learn the table numbers) it was by accident, but it was a perfect table with a lovely view of the famous water show in front of the hotel.

One night while dining, I observed an older couple at Table 1; they were dressed in tuxedo and gown. I occasionally picked up the tab for other diners, so I asked the waiter about this couple and learned they were celebrating a significant wedding anniversary. "OK," I said, "put their check on mine, but don't say anything to them until I've left." When I got up to leave I stopped at their table and congratulated them; they were quite moved that a stranger would make that effort.

"Sir, you're a pretty lucky man tonight," I said. "One, you've got this beautiful woman here with you. And two, you're lucky I'm not a thousand years younger, because if I were I would take her from you tonight."

They just loved it.

A few months later I returned to Table 4. Lo and behold, at Table 1 sat a young couple in tuxedo and gown. I called the same waiter over and asked what was going on. "They just got married." I could tell they were young and immature, not well seasoned for the world. Again I said, "Put their check on mine, but don't tell them."

When I got up to leave, I went by and congratulated them. I reminded the young man, "You know it's a lot of work to make marriage work."

"Yeah, yeah," he blushed. "I know." The young woman was giggly and red-faced as well. They were trying so hard to appear grown up.

I said, "You know, you're a lucky man tonight, fella. You've no doubt got the prettiest lady in all of Vegas."

He was bashful. "Yeah, I know."

"But you're lucky in another way. You're lucky that I'm not a thousand years younger or I would take her from you tonight."

They really liked that.

After myself going through two divorces—one of my own choosing, the other not—I appreciated both couples. The love that a young couple starts with, and the dedication and commitment that is demonstrated by the elder. How wonderful their marriages were to see. And how content I had become with my own life. It took me many years to work through the emotional turmoil of my second divorce, and God and school and art were all a part of the process. The remarkable thing was that I finally became *me*.

I became me, and it was the best thing ever.

WOULDN'T HAVE MISSED IT
FOR THE WORLD

In 2013, I decided it was time to sell my business. I'd loved the restaurant world for over fifty years, but an accumulation of economic circumstances made it harder and harder to continue successfully. It was an agonizing choice, a bittersweet moment, but as with many things in life, if we don't second-guess ourselves, we realize we made the right decision. In hindsight, selling the business was indeed the right decision for me, but I wouldn't exactly say I've retired. I'll always be busy—discussing art with friends, playing the piano, visiting the beach house, searching for additions to my various collections—though perhaps at a slower pace.

My newfound free time gave me a chance to reflect: I'd been through two divorces and two near-bankruptcies; I'd quit school at nineteen and returned at fifty; I'd had four wonderful children; I'd traveled the world and collected notable art. I'd experienced more success that I ever thought possible for a boy from Possum Trot. As Frank sang, "Regrets, I've had a few, but then again, too few to mention." It was time to consider what few regrets

I needed to lay to rest and what remaining dreams I wanted to fulfill.

I'd always regretted not knowing more about my extended family; my parents' reticence to share personal information always bothered me. Late in my life the mystery of my mother's family history was finally unveiled. I knew growing up that my mother was adopted, and I knew she had two brothers—my Uncle Bill and Uncle Clarence—but I knew little beyond that. I learned my mother's story from my cousin Bob, Uncle Bill's son, who has become the family historian.

My mother was born to James Andrew Widener and Hattie C. Harman in 1905 in Watauga County, North Carolina, near the Blue Ridge Mountains. She was christened Sallie Lucinda Belle Widener, apparently after the many Lucindas and Belles in her mother's family. She joined two older brothers, Clarence and Bill. Hattie's brother, William Harman, was a doctor in Springfield, Missouri; the whole family moved from North Carolina to Springfield, presumably to be closer to him.

When my mother was only a year old, Hattie came down with pneumonia. A woman, whose name I never learned, was brought in to help care for the three young children during their mother's illness. In the early 1900s, with limited medical treatment available, pneumonia was still one of the leading causes of death.

Hattie died in 1906.

After Hattie's death, my mother's father, James, took up with the woman who had been caring for the children and subsequently married her. James had arranged, without telling his new wife, that while they were on their honeymoon his three children would be adopted by local families. The new wife had grown to love the children while caring for them as Hattie lay on her deathbed; though his new wife was distraught, James would not tell her where the children were.

Bill was adopted by the Vetter family; my mother and Clarence were adopted by the Watson family. The Watsons changed my mother's name to Geneva Mae Watson. The boys' last names were changed, but they retained their first names. While I myself had chosen to change my own last name as an adult, I had to wonder how it would feel to have someone else change my entire name for me. I imagine the Watsons thought Sallie was so young she wouldn't realize her name had been changed, though it puzzled me nonetheless. Wouldn't her brothers still remember her original name?

According to my cousin Bob, it appears both families treated the children with love and kindness, which for their sake I was relieved to hear. I never met the Watsons (they died before I was born), but nothing my mother ever said led me to believe she had anything but the fondest memories of them.

Despite having been adopted by different families, my mother remained close to her brother Bill, but Clarence eventually dropped out of sight. Apparently over the years my mother tried to locate him but never succeeded. I have heard of cases where people want to be left totally alone. It seems to me as though they've been wounded somehow and want to punish themselves or others. For what other reasons would someone want to remain so isolated?

The evasive responses I received when asking about my biological maternal grandparents never changed, so I was shocked when I learned that my maternal grand-mother, Hattie, was buried in Springfield, only thirty minutes up the road from Walnut Grove. When I found this out—as a grown man, my mother long gone—I felt angry and upset. Why had my mother never mentioned this? Even if I never had a chance to meet my biological grandmother, I could have had a stronger emotional connection to her. I could have visited her grave, if nothing else.

My mother's lack of communication frustrated me. For a while I wondered if she herself didn't have this information, but there is a photo of my mother in her twenties that has *her* grandmother in it, as well as a photo with her mother's brother, the doctor in Springfield. So she *must* have known. Even if she were an adult before she learned the story, someone must have told her.

Maybe my mom's reluctance to share her history was her way of dealing with her mother's death and her father's remarrying and giving up his children for adoption. Perhaps she was so hurt that she turned her back on the past and gave her allegiance to the Watsons. I don't try to figure it out any more. It was her life, and she chose to live the way she wanted—just as she let her children live their lives the way they wanted.

When we found Hattie's headstone, I felt it was too small to give her the recognition due a young mother who saw her life slip away too soon. I'm replacing it with a larger, more befitting stone, and we conducted a family memorial service nearly 110 years after her death.

As for my mother's father, James? All we know is he died in 1936 in Kansas—and that's probably enough.

The mystery of my mother's first marriage and divorce was never unveiled, and Dorothy, my half sister from that marriage, never did become close to me or the rest of my siblings. Though we communicated periodically, she stayed within her social realm in Springfield. Yet, she does not deserve to be judged on whom she married and the benefits that came with the package, only the attitude that accompanied it.

Dorothy's struggle with alcohol overshadowed much of her life and brought grief to her husband, Richard, along with damage to their marriage. Dorothy told me there were many times she couldn't remember parking her car in the garage. My brother JE told me she called him one night to come and get her at a poker game because she was too drunk to drive home. I never heard exactly when Dorothy hit rock bottom, but she joined

Alcoholics Anonymous and became sober for more than twenty-two years until she died of cancer.

The cancer came quickly. She had been experiencing low back pain and attributed it to swinging the golf club. This discomfort continued for several months until the pain became so bad that she could no longer tolerate it. After an office examination, Dorothy's doctor told her she needed to enter the hospital for further testing.

While she was in the hospital, I called her each day to offer words of encouragement and to let her know she was in my prayers. One day on the phone she said something I'll never forget: "I'm never going to get out of here alive."

All I could say was, "You don't know that for sure."

Eventually the news came back: the cancer had spread to other parts of Dorothy's body and was not treatable.

From what I saw, she kept a positive attitude. Whenever I called, she would ask me how I was doing. Toward the end of her life, I went to Springfield and stayed for several days so I could visit her often. During one of my visits to her room, she said, "I told you I wouldn't get out of here." I just listened. What could I say at this time?

While Dorothy lay in the hospital dying from cancer, she displayed an unbelievable amount of courage.

Richard asked her one day as he stood by her bedside, "Would you like for me to bring you a highball?"

Without hesitation and without any discussion on the matter, her answer was precise and to the point. She said with great firmness, "No!"

In this one act, as if it were her final scene in a play, Dorothy showed conviction and commitment.

The story almost knocked me off my feet. Over all those years, I never really knew my sister, but I don't think I had ever respected anyone as much as I respected her at that moment. She could have justified taking a drink by telling herself, "What difference does it make now?" She was on her deathbed, but staying sober was what she stood for. In my opinion, she died with her boots on.

Dorothy's story caused a great paradigm shift for me. I saw her differently, and I saw myself differently. I saw courage and conviction in a new way, and I saw other things about life more clearly. On our deathbed, everything we work for and enjoy, all the things we covet and cherish, suddenly take on new meaning. The things we thought made us who we are suddenly become unimportant. Now we're forced to get real. No more games. We see life as it really is. If you miss this part of life, you've likely missed the best part.

Though I was never close to Dorothy until the end of her life, I kept in regular contact with the rest of my siblings — Ellene, Bill, Lawrence and JE. Ellene and JE stayed in Springfield, Missouri, and I visited regularly. Sometimes Bill and Lawrence and I would coordinate trips so we ended up at JE's house on the same day.

Whenever we were together as a group, it continued to be a jovial occasion. Several times my brothers and I went to a Par 3 golf course for a little sibling competition. Generally JE, a natural athlete, finished in first place and I came in a close second; Lawrence usually ended up in the frustrated position.

Friday night the entire family would gather at JE's house for cooking on the grill. We totaled about thirty counting all the kids running around, jumping in the pool and throwing the ball in the backyard. JE was a good cook; it was always a hit when he made my mother's famous Ice Box Pudding. (To this day, the recipe remains a family secret.)

After a filling meal, we would sit or stand around the kitchen counter swapping stories. The same story with a slight variation would still get the same deserving laugh as at every previous telling. Before long we'd move to the enclosed sun porch or the living room. It didn't matter what room we ended up in—we were bound to get down to the cow-tipping tales and stories of other crazy behavior.

While my siblings gave narratives of our growing up, I spent more time listening than sharing. I made comments that fit into the storyline, but I was careful not to come across as uninformed or trying to fit in with the big boys. Even at our older age I still wanted their respect and acceptance. I often resorted to humor.

As a child, the words I heard most often from them were "You're too young and too little, so you can't go."

As we got older they continued to say that to me in fun. One time we had all gathered at JE's house, and my sister and I were running to the store. My brothers asked where we were going in a tone that implied they wanted to go, too. I told them, "You're too old to go!"

On some trips to Springfield I spent more one-on-one time with Ellene. We would go to her favorite place, Silver Dollar City, near Branson, Missouri. She wanted only me to take her, and we would spend hours there. I loved buying her porcelain collectibles and sharing laughter. Her five kids turned out to be wonderful adults, and we keep in touch when we can. (They think I am "it," and I'm not going to tell them they're wrong!) Ellene, my sweet "Sis," remained close to my heart even when at a distance. From my gentle sister I learned to be kind and strong and to forge ahead. When she died from a brain tumor, I cried for a long time. Ellene was my second mother, and I miss her as much as if not more than Mom.

My brother Bill had a good career as a salesman. Even as I boy I had great respect for him in business. While a job in sales did not appeal to me, I did want to emulate his success. He was intelligent and personable and earned good money, but did not manage his money well. Through a couple of marriages and divorces and lack of financial planning, Bill ended up living in a modest apartment with no savings. When he died, I paid for his funeral. I didn't expect that sort of life for my brilliant older brother who mentored me on top of the coal shed. Watching Bill's situation through the years influenced my own habits with money. Business taught me to manage money closely; seeing people have so much and lose it all added an extra layer of caution.

Lawrence, my grade-school caretaker, and I remained close. He continued to be kind and thoughtful toward others, and he loved his three daughters and grand-children. Lawrence and I often traveled together, always laughing, always cutting up. I learned a gentle and less demanding side of life from him, and I always felt special around him. Lawrence and Ellene are the two people I miss most in this world.

My brother JE stayed his abrasive self throughout his adult life. He was in sales for many years and then worked as a substitute mail carrier, but he seemed only to complain about work; he never seemed satisfied. While I loved him, I found it difficult to be around him for very long as an adult. His attitude brought back too many childhood memories of being tormented by him; that wasn't the kind of life I wanted to dwell on. But life's trials and age have taught me some wisdom and sympathies for human frailty, and though I can't understand what drove JE, I recognize something must have tortured him for him to struggle so much.

Whatever foibles or failures we had as individuals, we were a close family and shared much love. My siblings have been departing this earth as they joined it, oldest to youngest; I'm the only one left.

My mom, my sister Ellene, and my brother Bill are all buried in a cemetery in Republic, Missouri. There was one extra family plot available, so I staked my claim by having my headstone placed at the gravesite. The stone is completely engraved except for the date of death. My epitaph is not a Longfellow quote or anything poetic; it's simple and to the point: "Cheeseburgers and Cigarettes Have Hastened My Demise." However, the longer I live, the less that statement applies—and I'm far more willing to change my epitaph than to live a shorter life just to prove the saying true!

Recently, one of my remaining dreams came to life. I had long dreamed of speaking at my high school reunion. At age seventy, I was asked to be the honored speaker.

While I had been back to Walnut Grove many times over the years, this particular visit forced me to view my hometown through a new lens. It felt like coming home from a two-week vacation to notice the aged look of the carpet in the living room and the need for a fresh coat of paint in the kitchen. As I wandered the quaint town that Marshal Fagan had so diligently patrolled, I saw the businesses had long ago died with the owners, and the buildings were crumbling. It seemed to signify the end of an era, to symbolize the loss of the family I grew up with. I never thought the impact would be so great, but no one is left to chat with about family history or to answer questions like "Do you remember Silas Sanford who lived out east of us?"

On this visit, I had the chance to go through the house I grew up in to see what the various owners had done to it. The biggest changes were downstairs. The ten-foot ceilings had been lowered to eight feet, and the large ornate doorframe molding had been replaced with new, too-small trim. One of the owners had enlarged the kitchen by knocking out the walls between the kitchen and the old bathroom and pantry. No more slop bucket, no more spice cabinet with parked gum. A new bathroom had been added off what would have been the dining room, and—miracle of miracles—it had running water!

Upstairs the floors that had chilled our feet on winter mornings were covered in wall-to-wall carpet, and a door connected the two back bedrooms where Bill and Ellene had slept. My bedroom still had the old marble doorknob that I'd stuck on the door when I was a teenager.

Outside there was no more hog trough, no more chicken coop, no more coal shed. Back when my mother sold the house, the new owner cut down all the trees in the yard. It made my mother heartsick—all those beautiful trees that took so many years to grow and offered shade in the hot summer. But the maple tree across the road still stood. I never stopped dreaming, and that tree was always there in my mind as I imagined success.

And I was here in Walnut Grove to share how my dreams had come true.

As I sat on the stage waiting for my turn to address the alumni, I couldn't help but think about growing up in Walnut Grove. I remembered riding my bike around town and my stunning insight into my future. I remembered the accounting classes I'd breezed through and the shop class where I'd welded the lockers shut. I remembered hitting the principal in the head with the orange.

I thought about Mr. Jim Cummins, my speech teacher and my only high school teacher still alive today. He'd been such a support for me and had done so many good things for Walnut Grove over the years. I'd been privileged to get to know him as an adult, and I wanted to honor him by making this speech.

I thought about all the years of hard work that had led me to this minute. I was scheduled to be the last speaker, the anchor, and I knew how special this moment was in my life.

Finally, I heard Jim Cummins read my introduction. I walked out on the stage fifty-three years after I had graduated from high school and felt the same thrill I did performing in my high school play.

I began my speech...

In high school one of my teachers, Mr. Jim Cummins, piqued my interest in plays. I love reading plays, and over the years I have put together a nice collection. One of my favorites is *Elsewhere*. In one scene a father and son are seated at a 45-degree angle to each other. A lone light shines from above. The audience is at a hush.

Slowly the son turns to the father. "Dad, I'm thinking about getting a divorce." The father says, "What? You've only been married a little over a year!" The son replies, "Dad, you've done nothing but complain about Mom for years. Why don't you go elsewhere?" The father leaps to his feet and says, "Because there is no elsewhere."

There is no elsewhere. We deal with where we are. There is no elsewhere.

Outside those doors are sidewalk stones for all the past graduates of Walnut Grove High School. Each graduate's name is chiseled in stone with the date and the class motto to serve as an inspiration and direction into the future. Those stones and Walnut Grove gave me everything I needed for my future.

Outside those doors the sidewalk stone speaks from 1962, the year I graduated. *You get out of life just what you put into it.* That proved prophetic to me over the years. Outside that door the stone speaks from 1994: *Success is a journey and not a destination.*

I began to tell the story of growing up in Walnut Grove. I told of dreaming under my maple tree. I told of my bike-ride inspiration and how it set me off on my wonderful journey to success — and how the journey itself has been the most wonderful part.

Outside those doors the sidewalk speaks from 1970: *The journey of a thousand miles begins with the first step.*

124

I told of leaving Walnut Grove with twelve dollars in my pocket, with the determination to work hard and become great. I told of taking that first step and leaving behind my mother, my family, the safety and security of home.

I left behind the smell of moist air coming down the alley from locker plant's refrigeration. I left behind the smell of denim in the Jones Brothers' dry goods store, the squeaking pine floors at Brim's Hardware and the slamming of the screen door at Glaze's Market. And who can ever forgot that cherry phosphate and limeade at Kenny Wheeler's drugstore?

But over the years I've come to think of Walnut Grove as my neighborhood. A town where everybody knew everybody else, but also a town where everybody looked out for one another. This is a great neighborhood. I've always loved Walnut Grove.

Outside those doors the sidewalk speaks from 1953: *We climb the ladder we build.*

I told of keeping my word and of working hard, from mowing lawns to delivering newspapers to driving in the hayfields and cleaning out stalls in farmers' barns.

Outside those doors the sidewalk speaks from 1967: *The door to success is labeled PUSH.*

I described my seventy-hour workweeks with excellence as my goal, how I woke up every morning eager to do what I loved in the restaurant business: satisfying customers.

Outside those doors the sidewalk speaks from 1956: *To strive, to seek, to find, and not to yield.*

I described my health crises, driving myself to the hospital, hearing "We're losing him" and still not giving up. I didn't change my goals; I didn't change my direction.

Outside those doors the sidewalk speaks from 1984: *Knowledge is the wisdom of all good things.*

I told the story of dropping out of City College at age nineteen, and of returning to Southeastern at fifty, all the while managing my restaurant business. I told of how glad I was to have completed my degree and the joy the experience gave me.

Outside those doors the sidewalk speaks from 2005: *Before you can be old and wise, you must be young*—and foolish, I might add.

And I had so many stories of foolishness, it was hard to choose what to tell—the story of hitting Principal Edmonson with the orange? the pound cake at Petrini's? the toilet-seat-cover bibs? I told all three stories and shared how foolishness had taught me wisdom.

Outside those doors the sidewalk speaks from 1965: *Reaching for the stars.*

I told of my joy in life. I love living on the edge and learning new things. Life doesn't pass you by; you watch life go by. I encouraged the audience to do what they love.

The sidewalks speak to those who listen. Although I left Walnut Grove, it never left me. I return today with more than twelve dollars in my pocket, but I come back with something far more important. I come back with a message: wherever you go, take Walnut Grove with you. Value what you have here; it's a great town.

This last sidewalk stone, from 1986, is about my life; this is about what I wanted you folks to hear: *Wouldn't have missed it for the world.*

Is that not about the best thing you could ever think of? I wouldn't have missed this journey for the world. And that's how you should feel at the end of every day, and I pray you will feel that way at the end of your life. It's never too late. *Wouldn't have missed it for the world.*

I closed then and I close now with a poem by R. Lee Sharpe.

Princes & Kings

Isn't it strange how princes and kings,
and clowns that caper in sawdust rings,
and common people, like you and me,
are builders for eternity?

Each is given a list of rules;
a shapeless mass; a bag of tools.
And each must fashion, ere life is flown,
a stumbling block, or a Stepping-Stone.

ACKNOWLEDGEMENTS

I love my life. At times I don't want to go to bed because I don't want my day to end. (I make up for it by getting up before 5:00 a.m. each day.) Sometimes I become so happy, I can't contain my joy. I have spent my entire life being happy and thankful.

I am especially thankful for all the mentors I've had over the years, including Jim Cummins, my high school speech teacher; John, Gino and Julio Petrini, the owners of Petrini's restaurant; Sam Battistone, Sr., cofounder of Sambo's restaurant chain; and the cofounders of the Golden Corral restaurant chain.

To Jackie Sawyer: you are my prayers answered!

I am grateful to my saintly editor (and therapist), Karin Wiberg, for helping me complete this book. Any mistakes in dates, events and names are mine, not hers.

I also offer my gratitude to Alan Hoffler, my speech coach, who helped me structure and prepare for the presentation to my alumni association.

Most important, I want to thank my family—those who are still here and those who have gone before. I miss my parents and siblings dearly, but I am blessed to have four children, three grandchildren and many cousins, nieces and nephews still with me. I have said little of my children and grandchildren in this book, in the hopes of shielding them from any public scrutiny, but it does not minimize their role in my life today. I love them, and I am grateful for their presence.

When I sum up everything in my life, I wouldn't make any part different. The total of one's life is an account of who you really are—how can you dismember any part of yourself?

An unknown poet once said:

> *Life itself can't give you joy,*
> *Unless you really will it;*
> *Life just gives you time and space,*
> *It's up to you to fill it.*

I've been so blessed to possess that wisdom and to do all the things I have in my life. None of it would have happened without my CEO, God. He has truly allowed me to reach for the stars.